PowerBranding™

Building Technology Brands
for Competitive Advantage

Marty Brandt

Grant Johnson

 IDG
INTERNATIONAL DATA GROUP IDG Thought Leadership Series

PowerBranding™
Building Technology Brands for Competitive Advantage
Copyright © 1997 by Marty Brandt and Grant Johnson

Published by
International Data Group, Inc.
505 Sansome Street
6th Floor
San Francisco, CA 94111
415-676-3000

ISBN 0-9656841-0-5

Design and layout
Mari Nakamura Design, Emeryville, CA

Contents

About the Authors

Marty Brandt

Marty brings a strong strategic and creative perspective to the brand-building challenges faced by technology companies. He's been passionately involved in positioning, marketing, and advertising major brands and new products for nearly 20 years. Marty started proBRAND in 1993 to help technology companies better understand, manage, and leverage brand equity for competitive advantage. He is also co-founder (along with IntelliQuest) of Brand Tech Forum, and was the director of the first Forum in 1993.

Formerly, he was the senior marketing communications and advertising executive at Sun Microsystems, where his responsibilities included global, integrated brand-building programs. Prior to that, he was with Chiat/Day, where he developed advertising and direct marketing campaigns for Dell Computer in the U.S. and U.K.

Before turning to technology marketing, Marty was Senior Vice President with Ketchum Communications in San Francisco, working with both advertising and direct marketing clients. He came to Ketchum from Campbell-Mithun in Minneapolis, where he started in advertising after receiving a B.A. in Mass Communications from the University of Minnesota.

Based in Menlo Park, proBRAND clients include Intel, SAP, E-Stamp, Acer, Dell, Hewlett-Packard, and Logitech. Marty can be reached at (650) 854-4581 or at www.probrand.com.

Grant Johnson

Grant started his career in marketing at age five, when he began selling his old toys, repackaged as private-label "grab bags," to neighborhood children. His career in high-technology marketing, however, began in 1979, selling control-computer systems for Communications Manufacturing Company.

In the late 80's, Grant entered the PC market and worked for several major corporations, including AST, Epson, Kodak's Interactive Systems division, Symantec, and Toshiba's Computer Systems division. Grant's depth of technology marketing experience encompasses a broad range of hands-on positions in the areas of new business development, corporate marketing, product and brand management, product marketing, marketing communications, and strategic marketing.

Grant received his B.A. from the University of California in Santa Barbara, and his M.B.A. from Pepperdine University. An ardent marketing practitioner, Grant has written several articles on marketing. He also has created and taught a course in product management and marketing at the University of California in Irvine.

As president of Get Results, Inc., Grant helps companies get better results by executing more effective branding, internet, and marketing strategies. Grant can be reached at gejohnson@aol.com or at (949) 425-9060.

Acknowledgments

We thought about writing this book for a long time. After finally beginning in early 1996, we must have revised the outline nearly a dozen times, lulling ourselves into believing that we were actually making progress. But until someone said, "Yes, I think the industry needs a book like this and we will publish it," we really didn't get started. That someone is Peter Horan, President of IDG Marketing Services. Peter also provided the necessary resources and guided us through the book development process, and helped keep us focused with remarks like "Guys, I don't care exactly when you finish it, just finish it soon." Deadlines are, naturally, very inspirational, and we appreciate his ongoing support and occasional prodding.

We also want to acknowledge Kelly Conlin, President of IDG, who recognized the need for – and supported the ongoing investment in – exhaustive research on technology branding as a key part of IDG's *Buying I.T. in the '90s* research series. Scott Kleinman, Vice President of IDG Marketing Services, was a key content reviewer along with Peter, and he greatly assisted us by carefully selecting the most relevant research he could find to support several key points throughout the book. His manuscript suggestions also helped us improve clarity, flow, and structural integrity. Jackie Nakano, IDG's marvel of multitasking, was responsible for all the day-to-day activities involved in guiding this project to its completion, and coordinated all input from the various parties, enabling us to stay on schedule. Our editor, Jan Bell, greatly improved the precision of our concepts and corrected the sometimes mystical construction of our grammar.

Many others contributed, directly and indirectly, as well. The indirect contributors include a variety of individuals, many of whom are quoted in this book, whose passion for and promotion of this subject inspired us. To the many direct contributors (too numerous to name, but cited in various places throughout the book), we thank you for the time you took from impossibly overloaded schedules to talk with us. We especially appreciate the access that many of our interviewees gave us to their own branding challenges. Their insights and unique perspectives helped add dimension to key concepts and substantiated many of the beliefs and views that we subscribe to and present in the book.

And finally, we thank our loved ones for tolerating our consuming passion for this book endeavor and for understanding that the persistent lack of adequate sleep often results in mild irritability and the general inability to function like normal human beings.

Many people feel they have at least one book *in* them. What they don't realize is how much work it actually takes to get it *out*, in written form. As the adage goes, "Nobody likes writing; everyone likes having written." *Enjoy.*

Marty and Grant

January 1997

Introduction

Technology Branding: from Oxymoron to Business Imperative

Brand consciousness inside technology companies is rising dramatically. Many companies now view brand building as an important strategic endeavor, and some are regularly measuring the status of their brands, just as they continuously monitor other important barometers of business performance.

But this is a recent phenomenon. Throughout the 1980's, the phrase "technology branding" was viewed by most in the high-tech industry as an oxymoron. Branding was perceived as a soft, elusive concept with a subjective nature that didn't mesh well with the concrete nature of technology products and their abundant, tangible features. While technology companies were totally focused on engineering the next great product, there was little conscious effort put into building a strong brand and even less knowledge about how to do it. Besides, just building a better product was often enough to secure strong sales and market-share growth, so why worry about the brand?

By the early part of this decade, however, the market experienced dramatic change. Product life cycles were compressed to six months or fewer in many categories. Product choices proliferated, and previously distinct market segments, such as consumer electronics and personal computers, began to converge. Computers became more and more securely established as a routine part of daily life in both homes and businesses. Then, as if this weren't enough market upheaval, the Internet "happened," further accelerating an already rapid rate of change. In this new environment, claims of outright product superiority became less tenable, and it became clear that a technically elegant product alone was no longer sufficient. As technology consumers began perceiving many products within a variety of categories to be more or less the same, the importance of non-product attributes in the purchase decision, such as brand image, began to increase.

Along with this realization that customers were viewing product advantages as transitory, or more perceptual than real, came the understanding that brand strength could serve to "break the tie" in the purchase decision process, resulting in competitive advantage. But knowing that something needs to be done is a lot different than knowing how to do it.

Why PowerBranding™?

Technology products and companies have unique brand-building challenges. It's not sufficient or prudent to merely apply traditional consumer or packaged-goods branding practices to technology products and hope for the best. Such an approach falls short of fully addressing the distinct challenges confronting technology brands. Why is this so?

It's because technology products are vastly different from most consumer and packaged-goods products. By and large, technology products are still very complex and profoundly affect the business operations and efficiency of the companies which purchase them. And unlike many impulse-purchase consumer products, technology products have time-consuming, multiple-influencer purchase processes. Plus, product life cycles are measured in months, not years. As David Arnold says, "Unlike consumer products, technology products die young"[1] – thus every product is continually being replaced by a technically superior one. Yet the brand must somehow endure. To successfully resolve this paradox and address the other unique challenges that technology brands face are the reasons we wrote *PowerBranding*.

What We Hope To Accomplish in the Book

A lot has been learned in the past few years about building technology brands – and about what works and what doesn't. Innovative research has uncovered important learning that provides guidance for technology brand builders. This book will examine these key findings, illuminate the best practices, and delineate a comprehensive approach to building technology brands for competitive advantage. We'll explore what gets in the way of building technology brands, establish a framework for technology branding, and then map out the fundamental strategies and tactics that lead to strong brands.

Along the way, we'll point out the important differences between introducing a new product and launching a new brand, explore the trade-offs between building product brands and building the company brand, and examine how product and brand attributes play distinct roles in the buying process. We will also shoot down some of the prevailing myths of technology brand building, such as:

- Branding is really about running an *image* advertising campaign.
- Branding is too *ephemeral* and difficult to measure.
- Building great products *alone* will create a winning brand.
- Branding is something to worry about *after* the product is launched.
- You need a *large* budget to be effective.

We also hope to bring some clarity to the ephemeral and often misunderstood concepts of brand and branding. While the importance of branding is on the rise, the lexicon for technology branding is inadequate. Furthermore, the diversity of incomplete brand advice prevalent in the industry causes much confusion and gets in the way of effective brand building. Thus, we'll present new definitions to help companies better understand branding, offer insights to spur companies to rethink their approach to branding, and present a practical branding methodology that technology companies can begin using today to gain important competitive advantages for tomorrow.

Branding has finally moved from the "nice to have, if you can afford it" proposition to a business imperative for technology companies of all sizes. We believe that winning technology companies will be – or, indeed, already are – increasingly differentiated by how well they get on with the job of building and managing brands and leveraging brand equity.

For individuals and companies that possess the will and commitment to build and manage their brands successfully, we hope this book provides both the knowledge and the tools to turn your aspirations into reality.

1
Rethinking Technology Branding

We have also focused on the value of the Microsoft name itself, which has become one of the world's best-known brands. In a number of ways, we are using the brand to make a statement about our vision, our culture and our abilities.

          – MICROSOFT 1996 ANNUAL REPORT

We follow four basic strategies:
     1. Develop products quickly
     2. Invest in manufacturing
     3. Remove barriers to technology flow
     4. Promote the Intel brand

          – INTEL 1996 ANNUAL REPORT

As most technology companies are now discovering, branding is not an optional activity that they can choose to engage in or not. With every message, perceptions are reinforced or altered slightly. With every customer contact, certain expectations are met – or not. Every experience with the outside world shapes, in large and small ways, the feelings, beliefs, and opinions people have about products and companies. What other businesses have known for a long time is just now becoming obvious in the technology industry: branding "happens," and it happens every day. The only real choice companies have to make about branding, then, is to determine what to do about it. To what extent are they willing and able to manage and leverage their brands for competitive advantage?

As these annual report excerpts attest, the two most successful companies in the personal computer industry certainly believe they can sustain real competitive advantage through the strength of their brands. Today, Intel and Microsoft are investing hundreds of millions of dollars annually in what was once considered a dubious investment: building the company brand. Clearly, they are committed to managing and leveraging their brands. Yet, in spite of these powerful examples of two market leaders which have rethought and revamped their entire approach to branding, technology companies of all sizes are still struggling with the idea that successful brand building should be a corporate priority tantamount to the successful delivery of new products. Why is this?

Constant Change Gets in the Way of Technology Branding

One of the most compelling obstacles to building technology brands is the relentless pace of the information technology industry. It's become an industry driven by constant innovation and product life cycles measured in months, not years. "Speed is God," David Hancock of Hitachi said recently in reference to the company's goal to completely refresh its portable computer line every six months. The Internet explosion now compels companies to design business plans with expectations of investment recovery within the first three to six months following product introduction. Microsoft launched three versions of Internet Explorer in little over a year. And many on-line or Internet content providers are updating their "product" offerings almost daily. With this ever-changing landscape and the pressing emphasis on product launch, it's not surprising that brand building often suffers from a "there's no time for it now; we'll get to it later" mentality.

In addition, as David Arnold says, "Branding and innovation are almost opposites."[1] Branding, especially successful branding, is all about consistency and familiarity and *building* customer relationships over time. Innovation is all about interruptions in continuity and *replacing* existing products with something new and unfamiliar. So, understandably, it's very hard for many technology companies to focus on determining where they'd like their brands to be in a year or two when they're so immersed in constant change and rapid product obsolescence. They're hardly able to look beyond next week's product development schedule and anticipate competitive maneuvers. And yet, the irony is that all the day-to-day activities, programs, and messages that result from constant innovation – all those deliverables that support the products of today – are, in fact, building and shaping the brand that companies will have in the future. With every communication to the outside world, the brand is happening, whether or not a company chooses to focus on and consciously manage it.

A Product-Centric View of the World Is Limiting

There's another reason why the prominence of technology branding has been slow to emerge. Up until the early 1990's, the prevailing view was that the product was everything and brands didn't matter much. It wasn't that success was simple to achieve, but branding was viewed by most companies as a relatively unimportant marketing or marketing communications activity, not as an important business activity. If a company could build a better product, secure great reviews in the trade press and among key influencers, garner sales from early adopters, and, ultimately, generate market momentum, then why bother with the brand? This technology-centric mentality was a virtual mantra in the industry. Just keep delivering "new and improved" models and watch sales climb.[2] Thus, the notion of paying scant attention to the brand was prevalent, and the idea of adopting a systematic brand management system was virtually unheard of in technology companies.

In the early 1990's, however, the technology market rapidly matured and evolved. Product choices multiplied; channels and target audiences expanded, while product life cycles contracted; the Internet suddenly "happened," and entire markets began to collapse and explode overnight. Today, having the best product alone no longer ensures success. With this relentless pace of innovation, product advantages have become more fleeting: as soon as one company brings a new product to market, a competitor delivers something better the next day or the next month. It's now increasingly difficult to convince customers that one technology product is significantly better than another or that the perceived advantages will exist for very long.

Thus, the product-centric approach to marketing that worked best when the market was characterized by real, enduring product differences

– when technology by itself was the most important differentiator – is no longer adequate. Most technology companies understand that sustainable product advantage is elusive and that product differentiation alone is not sufficient to ensure ongoing customer loyalty and success. Increasingly, they are focusing on other means of differentiation, such as building brand strength.

The other limitation of a predominately product-centric view of the world is that it generally gets in the way of brand building, because brand building requires a customer-centric view. All too often technology companies are so in love with their products that they fail to bring the customer perspective into the planning process until it's too late. No longer is it practical (as if it ever were) to build an elegant product and *then* find customers willing to buy it. It works best the other way around: determine what the customer wants and then deliver it. Some companies, where brand and consumer consciousness are high, strive to be customer-focused from the beginning. Apple, for example, brought customers into round-table discussions during the early planning on the PowerBook design. This approach helped them build a product with highly desirable features and a winning design that, in turn, enabled the PowerBook to become a billion-dollar success within the first year. While Apple has experienced both fantastic success and disappointing failure throughout its company history, Apple's customer focus has resulted in a consistently high level of customer enthusiasm and enduring brand loyalty.

Apart from Apple's Steve Jobs and a few other early marketing visionaries, the predominately engineering-oriented individuals who started and led technology companies in the 1970's and 1980's were generally unfamiliar with and skeptical of the whole branding concept. Not surprisingly, many technology company leaders are still uncomfortable with branding, partly because branding is often a misunderstood subject – even in companies that are getting on with the job. Only within the past five years has a significant body of knowledge – hard facts – about the increasing importance of brands actually emerged. In addition, the market success of companies like Intel and Microsoft has further demonstrated the tangible business benefits of brand building.

The Irony of Brand Indifference

Even those who are more open to the concept of technology branding, however, tend to believe that brands – and the power of brands – belong more logically to the world of packaged goods, fashion, and various prestige-oriented products. This is probably because most of us have been conditioned to think of "brands" primarily as products made highly visible through television and glossy print media advertising. But the irony of this viewpoint is that technology products actually have higher branding potential than many other product categories.

This is due, in part, to their complex nature and the fact that they are rarely purchased based on impulse alone. Rather, because they can have profound influence on business and personal productivity, technology products are chosen quite thoughtfully – i.e. they are "considered" purchases. In addition, due to the depth of experiences and relationships that are ultimately possible between customers and technology brands, technology products are actually a much richer field to mine than many consumer and packaged-goods products whose brands are often built largely through expensive image-selling campaigns. Since technology customers are faced with such an overwhelming degree of product complexity and so many similar product choices, they are actually predisposed to branding: it's a way to make their decisions, and, consequently, their lives simpler.

Furthermore, due to the speed of product obsolescence, technology brands take on a significant role in helping to bridge products from one version or generation to the next. Continuity with the customer, therefore, happens more at a brand level than at the ever-evolving product level. How often does one hear the term "product loyalty" in this industry? Not often, because product loyalty, per se, can't really exist for very long when customers are faced with six-month product life cycles. The "brand" life cycle, on the other hand, lives on, as shown in Figure 1-1. That's why technology companies need to pay as much attention to managing their brand life cycles as they do to managing their product life cycles. When products and the brands they represent are properly managed and each successive product successfully transfers its short-lived "equity" to the more enduring brand, the overall equity of the brand increases.

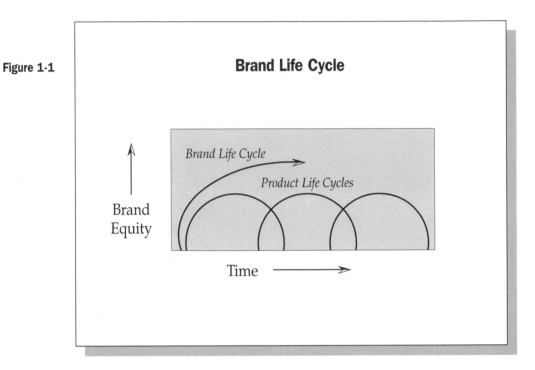

Figure 1-1

Brand Life Cycle

Brand Life Cycle

Product Life Cycles

Brand Equity

Time

That's good news, because it's our belief that strong brands and strong brand equity result in competitive advantage for technology companies. Strong brands can lead to greater marketing efficiencies in many areas, including more rapid new-product acceptance and easier market expansion. They can also result in higher selling margins, increased profitability, and more loyal, repeat customers. To understand how this works, let's start by defining, or perhaps redefining, a brand.

A New Brand Perspective

There are a variety of ways to define a brand. Some are broadly stated, some more limiting, and some more prosaic than practical. Here are a few notable examples:

- "A brand is a name." Joe Marconi, *Beyond Branding*
- "Brand is an icon with virtual memory." Regis McKenna, *Relationship Marketing*
- "A brand is a living memory, a genetic program, a contract." Jean-Noel Kapferer, *Strategic Brand Management*

- "A brand is a distinguishing name and/or symbol (such as a logo, trademark, or package design) intended to identify the goods or services of either one seller or a group of sellers, and to differentiate those goods or services from those of competitors." David Aaker, *Managing Brand Equity*
- "Brand is the personality or identity of a product, range of products, or an organization, derived from consumer perception of both tangible and intangible attributes." David Arnold, *The Handbook of Brand Management*

With so many different ways to define the single word that's at the core of this discussion, no wonder it's difficult to get on with the job of building brands. So here's our definition of a *brand* – one we believe makes sense for technology products and their unique challenges:

A brand is the tangible product *plus* the intangible values, associations, and expectations attached to the product by the customer or prospect.

These values, associations, and expectations are shaped, to varying degrees, by:

- Experiences with and around the product, both pre- and post-purchase
- Messages, controlled (yours) and uncontrolled (e.g. competitors, media, analysts)
- Perceptions and beliefs held by customers and prospects
- The technical knowledge and understanding of customers and prospects
- The basic technology itself
- Features and attributes
- Price

Here's an example of a brand:

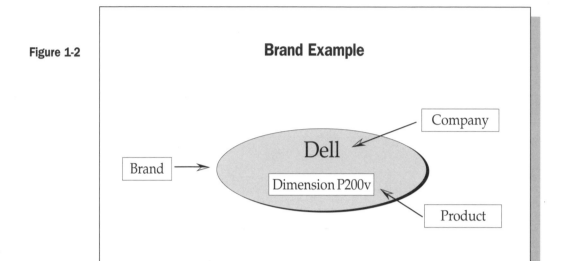

Figure 1-2

Brand Example

In this example, the product is a desktop personal computer that has certain features and attributes and is sold at a particular price. The company making the product is Dell. The *brand* – what someone actually buys – is the Dell Dimension P200v, and it encompasses the inseparable tangible product features plus all the intangible associations and values that are attached to the product by the customer.

A brand should not be confused with just the brand name, e.g. the *Dimension*. A name is certainly a part – a very important part – of the brand, but the brand is more. A brand should also not be confused with the brand image. The associations and perceptions – often irrational and emotional – commonly thought of as image are important components of the brand, but they, too, are not the entirety of the brand.

Again, we define a *brand* as the tangible product *plus* the intangible values, associations, and expectations attached to the product by the customer or prospect. Another way to think about this definition is in terms of the difference between the product and the brand:

Product = features + price
Brand   = features + price + name + identity + attributes + perceptions/associations

From this perspective, when we talk about brand we're really talking about something *inclusive* of the product, not separate from it. This is particularly important because many discussions about technology branding get sidetracked by the misleading argument over whether one should be marketing the product or the brand. The short answer is that both should be marketed.

Jim Garrity, Vice President of Communications for Compaq Computer Corporation, said recently in response to a question about how the company allocates dollars between product-oriented ads and brand-oriented ads: "We don't look at it that way. One of the elements of our strategy is that every product ad has *brand* features in it and every brand ad has *product* features."[3] This makes sense because technology purchasers do not consciously buy technology products without also considering the company that makes the product and the brand it represents.

Direct marketers like Dell and Gateway understand this concept very well. When customers purchase computer products over the telephone, they are buying a brand and its promise as much as they are buying a product. They are buying the reputation, identity, personality, and perception of these companies that "come" with their products. In fact, if you analyze Dell or Gateway's advertising, it's clear that nearly all of their ads, while having a clear call to action and a strong product focus, also contain ongoing messages about not only the company – its service, support, and other distinctive capabilities – but also its customers (e.g. "so many others choose us, shouldn't you?"). By constantly reinforcing both product capabilities and company or brand capabilities, Dell and Gateway engender customer trust and consistently build strong "brand bridges" from product to successive product. A resulting by-product of this conscious brand life-cycle management is that both companies continue to build equity in and preference for their respective brands.

Companies Make Products, Customers Buy Brands

As we have just described, the reality of how customers make purchase decisions supports our belief that, while companies *make* products, what the customer is ultimately *buying* is the brand.

What we mean by this statement is that product and brand are inseparable from the customer's perspective. As technology marketers, we may view tangible features and functions quite differently from intangible attributes, perceptions, and images. We may put such classifications into two distinct categories, one called brand and the other called product. Customers, however, don't make such a concrete distinction when purchasing technology products. They don't just buy a computer; they buy a Compaq Presario computer or an Acer Aspire computer. In this sense, the debate over brand versus product is moot. Both are important. Figure 1-3 shows how this "product/brand" relationship is viewed from the customer's perspective.

Figure 1-3

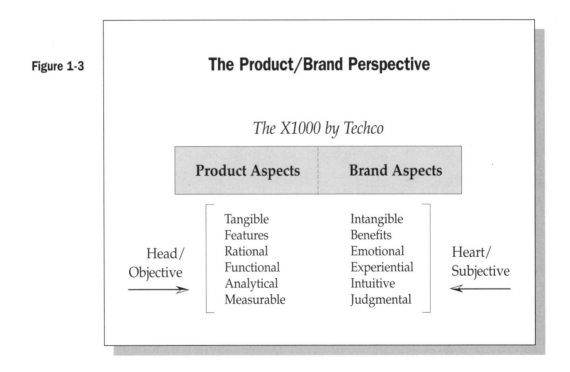

As this diagram illustrates, brands are a combination of "head" and "heart" aspects, tangible product attributes *and* intangible brand attributes. The brand management and communications challenge for technology marketers, then, is to determine the right combination or mix of messages to successfully position the brand to the customer. In some cases, it may be better to put more emphasis on tangible attributes related to technology or product features. In other cases, it makes sense to ensure that customers and prospects understand a company's strength in intangibles like service, dependability, flexibility, and stability.

The key to the issue of product versus brand is taking a look at it from the customer's perspective. No other perspective really matters. When it comes to dissecting brands, customers do not make the sorts of hard and clear distinctions that marketing and research people often do. Naturally, associations and attributes can be independently measured and ranked. But it's unwise to be lulled into thinking that they can be easily separated in the heart and mind of a customer—ultimately, the purchase decision made reflects both objective and subjective criteria.

A related customer-oriented approach to understanding the role played by non-product factors is to view the purchase decision from a broader perspective. As the "differentiation stack" diagram illustrates in Figure 1-4, today's technology vendors can't succeed on technology alone, no matter how sophisticated their products may be.[4] It takes much more to convince customers that a given vendor is the right choice, and that's, of course, where brand aspects or factors come into play.

Figure 1-4

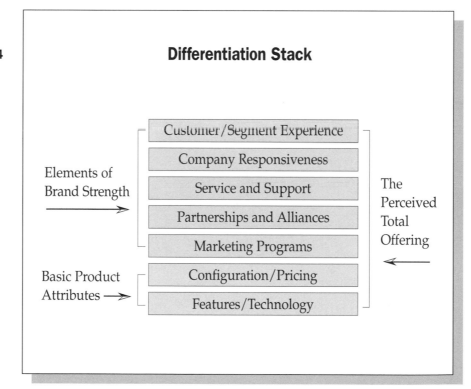

Differentiation Stack

Elements of Brand Strength →

- Customer/Segment Experience
- Company Responsiveness
- Service and Support
- Partnerships and Alliances
- Marketing Programs

Basic Product Attributes →

- Configuration/Pricing
- Features/Technology

The Perceived Total Offering ←

As the diagram illustrates, customers view product attributes in combination with a wide array of brand attributes that, together, can be called *"the perceived total offering."* In a customer's mind, the various non-product attributes, such as company experience, responsiveness, partnerships, alliances, service, and support, all influence how one vendor "stacks" up against another. Thus, one vendor's brand that is represented by much more than just the product can be perceived to offer a better "solution," even if the product alone is perceived at a competitive disadvantage. In this view, the perceived total offering is also a representation of a company's overall brand strength and, thereby, illustrates the power of the brand in influencing purchase decisions and creating competitive advantage.[5]

In summary, this chapter has explored historical inhibitors to the rise of technology branding, looked at the reasons why technology brands have high "branding" potential, provided a new "brand" definition, and examined products and brands from a customer-oriented perspective. In Chapter 2, we will turn our attention to a growing body of research that establishes the influence of brands in the purchase process for technology products, and also examine brand power and brand equity.

2
Brand Power and Equity

I think it's a great product...but it really was the brand.

      – WEBB MCKINNEY, Hewlett-Packard[1]

In technology, where products change rapidly, the brand is doubly important.

      – DENNIS CARTER, Intel Corporation[2]

Fierce debates are raging in the hallways of many technology companies. These are not battles over whether branding is an activity that companies should consciously engage in or not, because the belief that branding is important is steadily becoming widespread, although not yet universal. Rather, the debates are about whether to invest in building the product brand(s) or the corporate brand – whether to create demand for specific products or to create demand for the company as a whole.

In many ways, these debates are merely an outgrowth of a belief that is still prevalent in many technology organizations: build a better product, and customers will buy it. The drawback to this "product is everything" theory is that building a significantly better product and sustaining any real or perceived advantages for very long are now increasingly difficult. With shorter product life cycles, competitive product parity is the prevalent state of the technology market, and customers everywhere recognize this.

Naturally, every technology company continues to claim that it has the best product or solution, but, by and large, business and consumer purchasers alike now believe the "better product" throne is ephemeral at best and illusory at worst. Everyone knows that technology's advance is incessant – what's "breakthrough" today will be rendered obsolete tomorrow. So, in a practical matter, one is never really buying the best product, only the best product available *today*. Thus, increasingly, customers are looking to non-product factors when evaluating what products to purchase. This expansion in purchase criteria factors is demonstrated by a growing body of research that points to the increasing importance of company-level attributes (i.e. brand) in vendor selection.

Evidence of Brand Importance

During the past few years, research has disproved previously held beliefs that product attributes were all that really mattered and that brands were relatively unimportant factors in the purchase process.

In 1993, a study by IntelliQuest, a marketing research and consulting firm, indicated that "brand" or brand name was viewed as the second most-important attribute in terms of purchase influence (after "performance," but ahead of "price," "upgradability," and seven other factors).[3]

This same study examined the relative value of brands by posing the question, "If an IBM PC costs $2,000, what do the following brands cost?" The findings indicated that the premium a purchaser would pay for one brand versus another was significant, with the delta between the lowest and highest priced PC brands being $423 or around 21 percent.[4]

Then, in 1994, Wave V of *Buying I.T. in the '90s: Brand Power in Enterprise Computing*, an extensive research report conducted by International Data Group (IDG), asked respondents to score enterprise vendors like Microsoft and Novell on 11 different attributes (see Figure 2-1). These covered a range of brand associations falling into three broad classifications: product, function, and image. Further analysis of these attributes illuminated which had the most influence in determining whether a company was viewed as "strategically positioned" (see Figure 2-2).

Figure 2-1

11 Attributes for Company Ratings

Function Attributes
- Products Easily Integrated into Multivendor Environments
- Project Management and Integration Capabilities
- Products That Match Technology Solutions to Business Problems

Image Attributes
- Market Leadership
- A Company I Would Like To Do Business With
- Shares My Company's Vision for the Evolution of Technology
- Trustworthy

Product Attributes
- High-Performance Products
- Innovative Products
- High-Quality Support
- Reliable, Trouble-Free Products

Figure 2-2

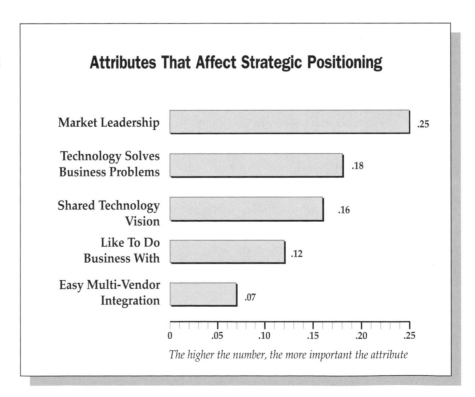

Attributes That Affect Strategic Positioning

Market Leadership .25
Technology Solves Business Problems .18
Shared Technology Vision .16
Like To Do Business With .12
Easy Multi-Vendor Integration .07

0   .05   .10   .15   .20   .25

The higher the number, the more important the attribute

As Figure 2-2 shows, not *one* of the top five attributes was a product attribute. Association with strong products and product attributes was only the basic requirement to get into the consideration set. Company or brand attributes, such as a company "I Like To Do Business With" or one that is perceived to have "Market Leadership," were most influential in determining whether a company was viewed as strategically positioned and, consequently, as a more desirable vendor. This research confirms the new reality for selling enterprise solutions in today's technology marketplace: strong products and product attributes are expected and only provide a technology vendor with an opportunity to compete for a customer's business. Overall vendor preference depends heavily on attributes that go well beyond the product.

This behavioral dynamic – where brand attributes exert significant influence in the purchase decision – does not just apply in the area of enterprise solutions. As the technology industry matures and more product categories become characterized by parity technology, having great products is becoming only the "entry card" for purchase consideration. It takes a lot more than strong product attributes to achieve differentiation in the customer's mind.

In 1995, IDG's *Wave VI* research report, *Brand and the Buying Process*, offered even more evidence of brand importance by quantifying the price premium that a strong technology brand could command. As shown in Figure 2-3, the price difference required to lead a customer to seriously consider switching to another brand demonstrated that one brand can carry a significant premium over another.

These premiums translate to brand strength in the marketplace and certainly impact the success of one product versus another, as well as the ongoing profitability or viability of one company versus another. In addition, a strong brand may even permit a company to experience delayed product introductions and still maintain its preferred position with current customers. Aaron Goldberg, Executive Vice President of Computer Intelligence, explains why this can occur: "In this industry, customers have extensive product-adoption cycles that reflect the significant time it takes for new technology to be fully deployed within an organization." Since companies upgrade technology over time and do not immediately convert to the latest and greatest products, this benefits

Figure 2-3

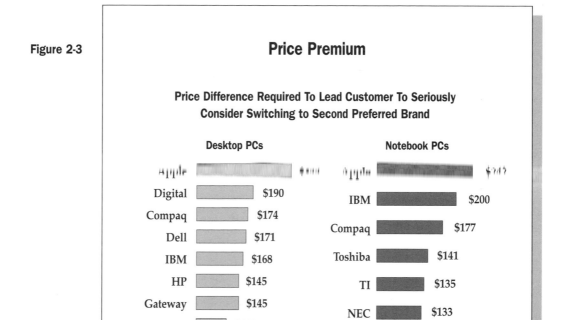

Price Premium

Price Difference Required To Lead Customer To Seriously
Consider Switching to Second Preferred Brand

their favored supplier (i.e. brand), that can occasionally be late to market with new product introductions and yet not miss out on new business opportunities.

Although, in some cases, companies may still lose some business (or customers) to more technologically advanced products, a strong brand name and a loyal customer base make it possible to regain customers and market share once the company returns to delivering products to market on time. Dell Computer Corporation, for example, has convincingly demonstrated this brand strength advantage by regaining significant share in the portable computer market segment, after nearly dropping out of the segment a few years back when its products were late to market.[5]

Brand Power

As this research indicates, brands are playing an increasingly important role in the purchase process for technology products. While brand influence to any degree is of interest to technology marketers, the relative degree of brand influence, or strength, of one brand versus another is even more insightful.

In *Wave V* of its ongoing series of global research on information technology products, IDG set out to measure the role of brand loyalty in the purchase process and the benefits of brand loyalty and brand strength in the personal computer marketplace. Entitled *Buyers and Your Brand*, this wave of research explored the relationship between customers and the specific brands of personal computing products they buy. In so doing, it uncovered a novel way to illuminate the strengths and weaknesses of brands.

By measuring the relative strength of individual product brands based on four distinct components, IDG came up with a collective measurement of brand strength called the *BrandPower™ Index*. The four components measured were:

- **Price premium**: how much more a buyer is willing to pay for one product brand over another similarly featured product brand.
- **Customer commitment**: how likely a buyer is to buy the same brand again and the willingness to go to any extreme to buy the preferred brand.
- **Brand advocacy**: the willingness of customers to play the role of brand missionary/advocate in the purchase process and the strength of their conviction (i.e. willingness to oppose a superior's decision not to buy a current brand).
- **Preference among non-customers**: ability to attract new customers to a brand.

Using this index, the study rated the top desktop and portable PC brands (see Figure 2-4). These ratings represent a composite of the four BrandPower™ components that were measured and thus reflect overall brand strength.

Figure 2-4

The BrandPower™ Index

Desktop PCs		Portable PCs	
Apple	74	Apple	71
Compaq	67	Compaq	64
Dell	65	IBM	64
IBM	64	Toshiba	63
Gateway	63		
AST	61		
Packard Bell	57		

However, a closer look at the individual components of the index provides insight into some of the key benefits of brand power. For example, *customer commitment* measured the percentage of customers likely to repurchase a given brand, as shown in Figure 2-5. This customer commitment percentage can also be viewed as an indicator of relative brand loyalty. In examining this particular measurement, one might ask why Apple, which demonstrated the highest customer commitment percentage, has experienced such a large decline in market share since the study was conducted. One reason is that *current* customer commitment does not necessarily result in an ability to win *new* customers. Another reason is that, while brand power (or equity) is a key driver of consideration for potential customers, even strong brand power cannot overcome the standards and market momentum disadvantages that Apple faces in competing with the collective power of all the "Wintel" (as the industry often refers to the Microsoft/Intel standard) vendors.

Another component of brand power is *brand advocacy*, which is demonstrated by a high percentage of customers who would actively lobby on behalf of a preferred brand. As Figure 2-6 shows, HP has a high percentage of customers willing to "stand up" for its brand and an especially high comparative advantage in the inkjet printer market segment.

Figure 2-5

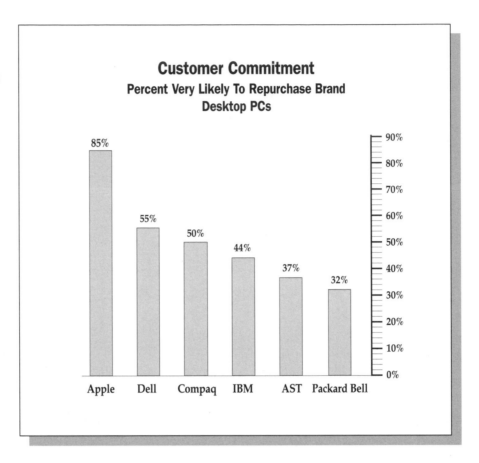

Customer Commitment
Percent Very Likely To Repurchase Brand
Desktop PCs

Figure 2-6

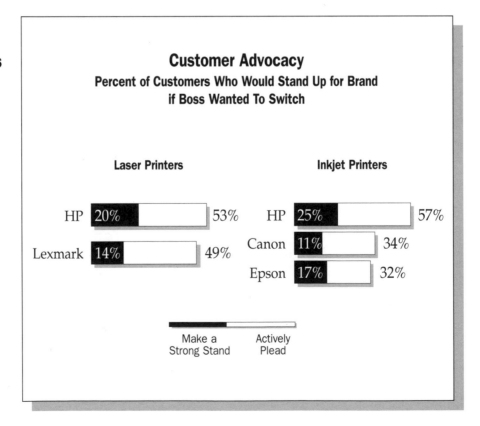

Customer Advocacy
Percent of Customers Who Would Stand Up for Brand
if Boss Wanted To Switch

While these components of brand power illustrate how some brands have greater power and leverage in the marketplace than others, they do not explain "how" they got that way. We believe that brands become strong by engaging in a series of systematic actions that all revolve around *consistency:* of product excellence, product quality, product delivery, customer service and support, communications, and many other aspects of business performance that, over time, result in providing something different *and* better to the marketplace. Consistency is a key element of *PowerBranding*, which is the "how" of building strong brands that we will explore in Chapters 3 through 9.

When and Where Do Brands Matter Most?

Given the dynamic nature of this market and the fact that both product-related and brand-related factors influence the purchase decision, it's reasonable to consider whether the influence of the brand changes or fluctuates based on where a product is in the life cycle or market maturity cycle, or on how experienced a particular customer may be with a given technology.

In his two books, *Crossing the Chasm* and *Inside the Tornado*, Geoffrey Moore presents a technology adoption life-cycle model, which explains the process by which technology products are able to "cross the chasm" and gain broad market acceptance. His model also illustrates what happens when products are unable to successfully "cross the chasm" and why such failures occur.

According to Moore's view, the importance of the brand in the purchase decision process varies in accordance with technology adoption life-cycle stages.[6] During the early market stages, when primarily "innovators" and "early adopters" are buying technology products, branding does not work well. Presumably, this is because these types of buyers are not concerned with the brand and care solely about how new technologies and products can increase company productivity and create competitive advantage.

This view has some merit, since it's difficult to leverage the company heritage when there isn't much of one, and it's hard to establish the company brand when it's in the formative stage. On the other hand, many new products that enter the early stages of market evolution are introduced by established companies with well-known brand names. One could argue that, in certain cases, without the strength of a well-known brand name, certain products would never succeed, even among early adopters, let alone "cross the chasm" into the mainstream marketplace.

Lotus Notes is a clear example of *brand* strength supporting the *product's* evolution. It took several years for Lotus to establish broad market acceptance for Notes. While it's true that Notes was able to successfully "cross the chasm," it's hard to believe that so many major corporations would have not only stuck with Lotus Notes through its several release versions, but also invested substantially during the formative years of the "groupware" category without the long-term product development commitment and financial stability of an established company like Lotus behind Notes.

As markets evolve, however, branding becomes more important, according to Moore. In the early majority stage of the technology adoption life cycle – where the market has grown to relatively high volumes and distribution channels are in place – the battle for market leadership intensifies. Companies race to continuously lower production costs and drive down price points, while they simultaneously increase product functionality. "More for less" is the mantra. And "eat your children before someone else does" is the mission, meaning that all companies in this life-cycle stage attempt to replace their current products with better ones as quickly as possible – before a competitor beats them to market. With so much thrashing occurring in the marketplace, it's understandable that customers begin to grow weary of endless product superiority claims and the difficulty of discerning ever-diminishing or fleeting product differences. Thus, according to Moore, the role of brand in influencing purchase decisions increases.

In contrast to this view that brand influence increases commensurate with market maturity is the view that brand influence can diminish based on customer sophistication or previous experience with a given technology. According to Aaron Goldberg, the "technical acumen" of the buyer can influence the role that brand plays in the purchase decision: "The more knowledge a buyer has about the technology and products they are

considering, the less they may be influenced by the brand." Novice
buyers with less product experience and less knowledge would, according
to this observation, be more influenced by the brand. Bruce Stephen, Vice
President for International Data Corporation (IDC) Research, offers a
similar view: "The novice buyer is likely to be influenced more by
recommendations of others, which tends to focus the purchase decision
on a few established brands and away from which product has the best
perceived features." Both life cycle and customer sophistication are
interesting brand theories that will require additional research in order to
determine how broadly they may apply to the current realities in the
technology marketplace.

The Components of Brand Equity

As research has clearly demonstrated, brands and brand power matter a
lot in the technology industry. And recently, as intensified pricing and
market-share battles place increasing pressure on company revenues and
margins, a newfound interest in both understanding brands and building
brand equity has emerged. But what is brand equity? It's a term and a
concept that's even more confusing than a brand. Many people tend to
think of it primarily in financial terms. For example:

> "Brand equity is the total accumulated value or worth of a brand; the tangible
> and intangible assets that the brand contributes to its corporate parent, both
> financial and in terms of selling leverage."
>
> – LYNN UPSHAW, *Building Brand Identity*

> "Brand equity is the financial and commercial value of the brand to the
> organization which owns and utilizes it."
>
> – STUART CRAINER, *The Real Power of Brands*

Financial World magazine, in its ongoing "The World's Most Valuable
Brands" report, also measures brands with the type of financial
orientation expressed in these two definitions.[7] While these views of
brand equity are important, they are also limiting because they tend to
be a backward-looking score of past events. So, while they provide
interesting comparisons between large brands or brands within particular

categories, they aren't helpful in providing companies with much insight into or direction for taking actions to build brand strength.

If brand equity is only presented as a "point in time" type of score or expressed solely as a numerical measurement, it will always be a difficult concept to grasp and make real to management. However, there is a way to make brand equity a more tangible and accountable aspect of your business. The secret to doing this is to utilize a practical approach which views brand equity as the sum of several components that can be separately identified and measured. Thus, if each component can be measured, it can be managed proactively in the context of ongoing business goals and ever-changing market conditions. And if brand equity is presented to top management as a pragmatic piece of the business success puzzle, it can then play a more prominent role in the day-to-day business decisions that ultimately impact brand equity.

With this in mind, our approach is to define brand equity this way:

Brand equity is the unique set of real and/or perceived distinctions attached to a brand *by customers*. These distinctions or differences between brands:

- Should (but not always) add value to and preference for the brand.
- Develop – and change – over time.
- Result from a wide array of direct and indirect experiences.
- Are generally measurable, but often intangible.

This broader view of brand equity is important for a few reasons. First, it says that brand equity is not one thing or one number but, in fact, a complex array of many things. Second, it says that these unique dimensions can each enhance brand equity and be reflected in the overall brand strength that is equal to, or potentially greater than, the sum of its parts. And third, it says that brand equity exists only to the extent of a customer's ability to make distinctions or recognize differences between brands.

These distinctions or differences between brands are manifested in seven primary dimensions, as shown in Figure 2-7.

Figure 2-7

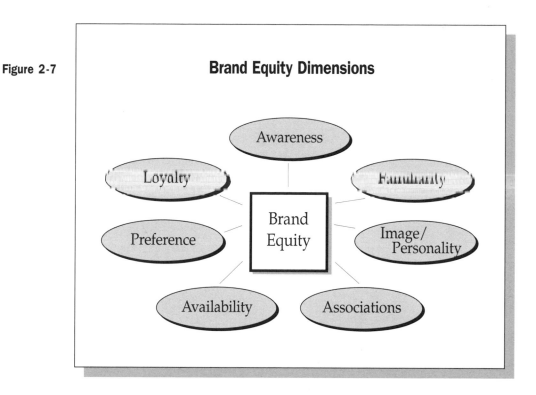

Brand Equity Dimensions

When you examine brand equity from these several dimensions, you are better able to understand and isolate where brand problems exist and where competitive advantages need to be reinforced. Again, it's important to point out that brand equity lives only in the hearts and minds of customers. So, if you're going to do anything about moving the needle in the right direction on any of these dimensions, you must have current and valid insight into the customer and the distinctions he or she makes about your brand versus competitor brands. Taking a holistic and integrated view of brand equity is also essential if one seeks to gain maximum brand leverage. Since all of these dimensions are interrelated, they must be managed with an eye on the entire spectrum of brand-equity variables. Otherwise, gains in one dimension could be offset by losses from mismanagement in other dimensions. Plus, only by looking at brand equity throughout all these dimensions can you accurately determine where key problems lie. Let's examine what each of these seven dimensions means and how each influences brand equity.

Awareness

One of the fundamental distinctions customers make about a brand is simply whether they are aware of it or not. Awareness, both unaided and aided, is widely used as one of the key measures of branding effectiveness. In fact, it might be argued that without awareness of your brand you have no equity at all. But brands with high awareness may not have strong brand equity. So, while awareness is the first step in selling any product, it's not the most important step toward building a successful brand. Rather, differentiation is the key to building brands. Of the different levels of awareness, unaided is probably the most meaningful because it reflects a customer or prospect's ability to recall your name spontaneously. In addition, awareness measures are more important in tracking new brands than established brands that often have challenges in other dimensions of brand equity.

Familiarity

Familiarity is important because mere awareness of your brand doesn't mean buyers understand much, if anything, about your brand's advantages or differences. We break out familiarity as a dimension of brand equity because it's really the key step to brand consideration. It reflects the salience customers attach to your brand. People tend to want to do business with companies and brands that become familiar to them.

Business Week recently conducted research about the importance of familiarity to information technology buyers. They found that almost seven out of eight buyers felt it was somewhat or very important to have familiarity with vendors of technology products. As one respondent put it: "I just feel better doing business with someone I know." This statement is a truism that applies to most purchases by businesses and consumers alike.

This is also one reason why it's difficult to succeed at component or ingredient branding. The opportunities to become familiar with a brand name or symbol are more limited when the brand is one of several components in a particular product, such as the graphics controller within a personal computer. It's hard to stand out without significant investment in high-visibility communications, and, unlike Intel, most component companies do not have the resources required to successfully establish their products as well-known ingredient brands.

Image and Personality

One of the most powerful dimensions of brand equity lies in the distinctions customers make about the image and personality of brands. This dimension is quite powerful because the minds of customers can contain a hodgepodge of feelings, impressions, and experiences that all play some role in their view and consideration of a brand. Brand image is an umbrella term that covers many different aspects of the total image, including product and company images. In recent years, brand personality has gained importance in the technology marketplace as a means of differentiation, especially as meaningful product differences in many technology categories continue to diminish. Some brands, like Gateway, Yahoo, Iomega, and Dell, have managed to create distinctive personalities for themselves. Other brands have virtually no personalities or the wrong ones, which can adversely affect their brand status.

Associations

Identifying the right associations and attributes for customers to attach to your brand is also key to building brand equity. It's critical to know with certainty what associations are important to customers, which ones your competitors already own, which ones are available to you, and, perhaps most importantly, which ones you can realistically deliver to differentiate your brand from the competition. Mature brands can be burdened by certain negative and enduring associations which take time and significant effort to change.

Abby Kohnstamm, Vice President of Corporate Marketing for IBM, said recently that IBM is working hard to diminish certain associations that it considers harmful to its core brand, including perceptions that it is "arrogant, slow, closed, proprietary, or sells hardware only." Over the past three years and after spending hundreds of millions of dollars on global communications campaigns, IBM has been successful in reducing the levels of these associations, but not in eliminating them. On the other hand, the company has also created powerful new, positive associations that have helped minimize the impact the negative ones can have on consideration for its brand.

Some brand associations, like reliability in the personal computer arena and dependability in the computer storage market, are basic market-entry requirements. These associations, however, are not necessarily highly differentiating, because all companies are expected to have such associations just by virtue of the product category. Other associations such as perceived quality are vitally important to have regardless of product category. Also, distinct associations attach independently to the corporate name, the product brand name, and even product components and ingredients. Collectively, all of these associations play a role in the brand-building process.

Availability

This dimension primarily refers to the ease of actually finding and buying your brand – in other words, its availability when a customer is shopping for or purchasing a particular product. Customers make judgments about and recognize differences between brands based on availability. If a company is able to achieve brand awareness or, even better, brand familiarity, yet does not have its products widely distributed and available where interested customers are shopping, neither sales opportunities nor brand equity are being maximized. In addition, just having the product available but not easy to find within a particular store (i.e. not having strong "shelf space" or prominent "product placement") can also diminish brand perception. That's why channel management is a critical component of successful technology branding.

Preference

Brand preference and selection happen when a customer weighs different purchase variables (both rational and emotional) and makes the ultimate distinction between brands – a decision to buy one brand over another or among several good alternatives. Preference over competitive alternatives is where brand building pays off. This is where conviction lives. It's the moment of truth. Which printer am I going to buy? What Internet service should I select? Am I going to stick with the Toshiba notebook or go with Fujitsu? After all the features have been compared, opinions gathered, and prices reviewed, there may not be much perceived difference among the various product choices. What's the tie breaker going to be?

Sometimes the decision is not completely rational. It could come down to which brand or company a buyer *likes* better. In fact, just liking one brand more than another often plays a key – but hard to measure – role in this preference dimension. Other important considerations being fairly equal, people have a strong inclination to choose the brand they feel is right for them. But traditional research will rarely uncover likeability as the reason given for a purchase choice. It takes a more innovative approach to determine how much people actually like doing business with you. Likeability, nevertheless, can play a key role and often make a difference in brand preference.

Whatever the key factor is, it's critical to understand what actually tips the scale – what drives preference and the ultimate purchase. Is it something different for first-time buyers than for repeat customers? If a sale is lost, why? These are all important questions that can help uncover exactly what drives purchase preference for one brand over another. In our experience, not enough companies actually research "lost sales" on a systematic basis in order to determine what they can do to change future consideration and win more sales. Even for some lower-priced products, like application software, analysis of lost sales can be quite revealing.

Loyalty

Brand loyalty is increasingly recognized as the most important dimension of brand equity. Larry Light, a leading brand consultant, asserts that brand loyalty is the marketing mandate of the 90's. He believes that brands are not an asset by themselves; they only become a valuable asset when there is loyalty to the brand. Brand loyalty is the payoff; it's the strength of customer commitment to your product. In addition, enthusiastic, loyal customers can be up to 10 times more profitable than other customers, according to Light's research.

There are two important loyalty dimensions: the actual buyer's *behavior* that is demonstrated through repeat purchases of the same brand and the *attitudes* and *feelings* about the brand, in terms of liking, trust, and confidence. Although there is a relationship between brand loyalty and customer satisfaction, they are not the same. Recent studies show that customer satisfaction does not necessarily lead to brand loyalty because customers can claim to be satisfied, as most do, and still switch brands at the next buying opportunity.

And, while brand loyalty can be a very powerful barrier to entry, one should not confuse loyalty with a situation where one is literally "locked in" to a particular brand due to high switching costs. For example, while internetworking products and operating systems software may appear to have strong brand loyalty, the ongoing allegiance to these products probably has more to do with high switching costs and other market factors, such as third-party support, than with loyalty.

Finally, brand loyalty may be the dimension of brand equity most impacted by the Internet as a channel of communication. Companies are already finding that the personal and interactive capabilities of the Internet are ideally suited for strengthening and nurturing the relationship between brand and buyer. As new technologies emerge for capturing data on – and purchase behavior of – individual customers, the opportunities for building brand loyalty "one customer at a time" may increase dramatically.

Brand Equity Caveat

One of the challenges in evaluating brand equity is to be able to separate brand-related factors from other market success factors, like technological advantage, distribution channel advantage, and the operational or implementation superiority of one company over another. As strongly as we believe that brands and brand equity matter, we recognize that in this industry a superior *technology* will often beat a superior brand.

Another way of looking at this dynamic is that brand equity makes a difference only when built on top of a solid foundation of competitive technology, effective distribution, efficient operations, and the right price/value product offering, as shown in Figure 2-8. Unless you have the business fundamentals in alignment with each other and with your competitive set, brand equity won't be the answer. Nevertheless, strong brand equity can provide some breathing room – and time – for companies to get their fundamentals back into competitive parity. Compaq's resurgence after a major setback in the early 1990's is an example of a brand whose strong equity provided a short-term buffer from competitive misalignment in major areas of its business operations.

The other caveat is that real product innovation and true product differentiation will beat brand equity nearly every time in this market. Customers are not dumb. When customers learn of a remarkable new product, they will not stay with the current leader just because of its strong brand equity.

Figure 2-8

Brand Equity Caveat

Brand Equity makes a difference only on top of a strong business foundation.

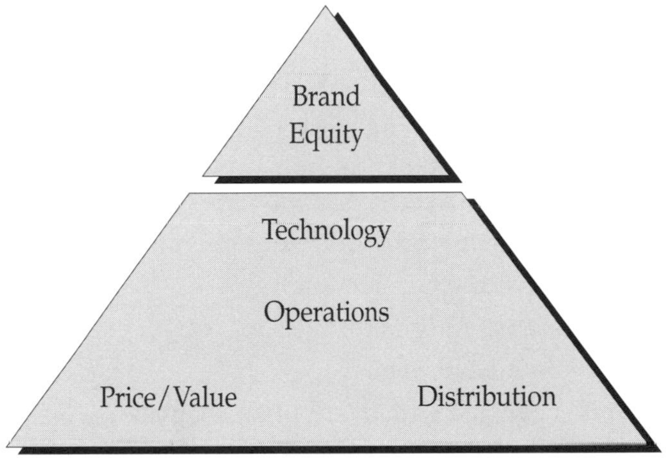

Brand
Equity

Technology

Operations

Price/Value   Distribution

Equity Happens

Clearly, if one looks at these seven dimensions of brand equity individually and collectively, there's a lot a company can do to affect each dimension and enhance overall brand equity. How, then, should a company best proceed with this comprehensive view of brand equity? First, determine what makes sense for your business. Every company should have a collective and corporate view of brand equity. If our approach is suitable, then use it. If not and a simpler view is more appealing, then utilize a different one that is better suited to your business. The key to making progress is to determine which metrics and measurements you have – or need to get – in order to answer two fundamental questions: what is our overall brand equity in the marketplace today – and what are the trends affecting it, either positively or negatively?

This is what a company needs to know because, ultimately, equity happens. It's happening today to your brand through the actions you're taking – or not taking. And inaction makes it easier for your competitors to build their equity at your expense. The challenge, then, is to proactively manage the process, rather than let your brand equity be largely the result of ad-hoc contacts, messages, and experiences. A comprehensive approach like the one just presented can help you step up to the brand-equity building challenge.

The need to consciously and systematically manage brands and brand equity is further demonstrated by a brief overview of the various concrete market advantages or benefits afforded by strong brand equity. Brand equity research and market outcomes in several industries have repeatedly demonstrated that strong brand equity can lead to:

- Higher margins or a price premium
- Increased consideration
- Increased opportunities for market expansion, segmentation, and brand extensions
- Leverage with distribution channels
- Marketing and sales efficiencies, especially in winning new customers
- Greater customer retention and loyalty (i.e. higher repurchase rate)
- Quicker new product acceptance

All these benefits of brand equity result in a competitive advantage that, like clear product differentiation, makes a difference in company profitability, market-share position, long-term corporate performance, and even stock market return, as recent research has demonstrated.

Brand Equity and the Stock Market

David Aaker, one of the leading authorities on brand equity, recently undertook a study designed to assess the relationship between brand equity and stock return. Aaker used three dimensions of brand equity:

perceived quality (a key brand association), awareness (in terms of salience or having an opinion about a brand), and brand loyalty. Using brand-tracking data from the EquiTrend measures of the Total Research Corporation, Aaker compared the results of 34 publicly held companies over three years. While this study didn't focus on the technology industry specifically, companies like Compaq and IBM were included in the sample. Aaker's study found that brand equity does have a significantly positive impact on stock performance. In Professor Aaker's words: "These results should be encouraging to those attempting to justify investments in brand equity, especially when tough questions are raised about the bottom line."[8]

Two Classes of Technology Brands

Not long ago, Stewart Alsop, one of the industry's leading pundits, declared that only a handful of technology brands actually exist – Apple, Compaq, IBM, and a few others. The rest, in his view, had not yet achieved "brand" status. While he may have made this declaration just to stir up a little controversy, many people still think that only large companies can build a brand. The fallacy of this view is that it assumes "brand" to be synonymous only with broad visibility and top-of-mind awareness.

A broader and more realistic way to look at brands is this: there are visible brands and virtually invisible brands; there are well-known brands and not so well-known brands; and, ultimately, there are successful and unsuccessful brands. Certainly, some commodity, component, or original equipment manufacturer (OEM) products are almost – but not quite – totally devoid of any brand element (since even these brands generally put the company name on products, they are still known, only to a smaller audience).

Therefore, to confer brand status on only the biggest, highest profile names misses the point. Branding is all about differentiation and added valued, as perceived by customers. Branding is about creating recognition and familiarity among key audiences, which in some cases is very limited in number. Practically speaking, then, there are two primary classes of technology brands – strong brands and weak brands. Naturally, all brands should be constantly striving to become stronger.

This chapter has presented significant research and evidence on the importance of brands in influencing the purchase of technology products, examined different approaches to measuring the power and strength of brands, and delineated the importance of fully exploring and managing brand equity. With this background, we will now articulate the "how" of technology branding, via an approach we call *PowerBranding*.

3

The Framework for PowerBranding™

Branding, properly understood, is virtually synonymous with marketing.

— DAVID ARNOLD,
The Handbook of Brand Management

Marketing is objective, intuitive and subjective.

— WILLIAM DAVIDOW,
Marketing High Technology

Not everyone today would go as far as Arnold does with his view on branding. And, had technology branding been popular back in 1986 when Davidow wrote those seemingly contradictory words in his classic book on technology marketing, he might have substituted the word *branding* for *marketing*. Yet both views express an understanding of the complex and subjective nature of branding. It's not an easy topic to understand or to capture in just a few pages, let alone a few words, which is one reason why many companies continue to resist facing up to their significant branding challenges.

In today's hyper-competitive marketplace, it's clear that the proper application of branding principles and effective practices makes a big difference in how companies perform. We call our approach on "how" to apply the appropriate principles and "how" to exercise the best practices *PowerBranding* (see Figure 3-1). It's our belief that this methodology can have a major impact on brand *and* company success.

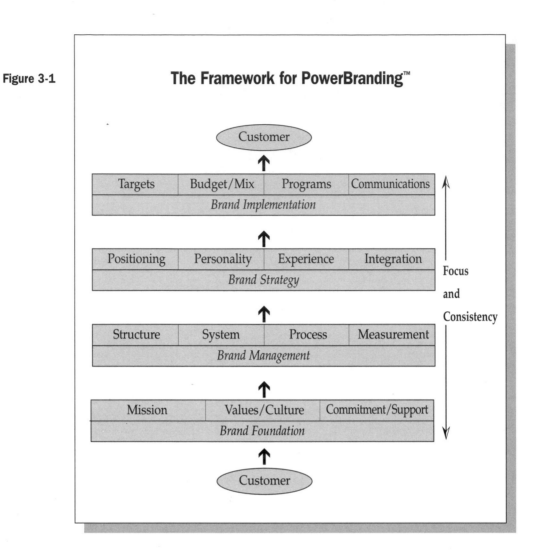

Figure 3-1

The Framework for PowerBranding™

The Framework for PowerBranding

What is this thing we call *PowerBranding*? First, it's a philosophy about branding, as well as a detailed, practical, and strategic approach to branding. It's thinking about and dealing with branding in a holistic fashion. It's having a brand management system to guide everything that involves branding. And, naturally, *PowerBranding* is the *power* of all *branding* elements working together effectively to build brand equity and competitive advantage.

In practical terms, *PowerBranding* encompasses four broad areas:

■ A corporate philosophy that starts with the belief that building brands is important because strong brands make a difference in business performance.

- A management process and system that supports brand-building efforts as a core business function.
- A set of strategic principles and a strategy to guide longer-term brand development.
- The practice and implementation of smart brand-building activities on a daily basis.

In this chapter, we will examine the first stage in this strategic approach to branding, i.e. establishing a brand foundation. Later chapters will explore the other key elements contained in the *PowerBranding* framework.

Establishing a Foundation and a Direction

The first step in *PowerBranding* is to establish the foundation and direction for building a brand or a family of brands. This foundation is not just about setting a goal or objectives. It's about articulating the broader and higher vision or destination for the brand, clearly expressing the brand culture and values, and establishing a high-level and fundamental commitment to building the brand. It's about Apple striving to be "the computer for the rest of us" with unwavering passion for innovation, quality, and challenging the status quo. Or Michael Dell's idea to not merely sell computers directly to customers, but to fundamentally "change the way people buy computers." Strong, enduring brands evolve from what is fundamentally authentic and differentiating about their products and the company that makes them. When companies take the view that "brand" is the expression of these fundamental truths about the company, good things can happen.

This basic step is absolutely critical to a brand's ultimate success. Yet, it is often overlooked or not done well, because it requires companies to embrace brand-building at fundamental or core levels of an organization, which is not something that many are prepared to do. But the foundation is where the groundwork for building a strong brand must begin. As we see it, three parts are key to this foundation for brand success: brand mission, brand values and culture, and commitment and support.

Brand Mission

All successful brand-building efforts begin with a clear statement of the mission or vision. Unless people inside an organization have an understanding of – and passionate belief in – the overall aim and purpose of the company, it's difficult to put together a coherent brand strategy or make effective tactical decisions along the way.

Successful technology brands reflect the excitement and commitment of the people within the organization who enthusiastically support the aspirations of that organization. Yet, there is often confusion about the semantics of mission and vision. We don't want to get bogged down with trying to convince you that mission is a better term than vision. Different business books provide different views and interpretations of these two words. Ultimately, it doesn't matter how you choose to interpret these terms. "Vision," "mission," and even "purpose" can be used interchangeably. The key is not in the word used but in how powerful, clear, and compelling the statements are.

If you don't know where you're going, you might end up somewhere else.

– Yogi Berra

In this sense, brand mission statements sometimes differ from business mission statements. Business mission statements that tend to deal with typical, yet important, issues like quality, leadership or customer satisfaction are often limited in their ability to inspire extraordinary brand-building efforts. For the purpose of defining a proper brand mission, several guidelines work for us. A mission is a fundamental goal of an organization or the reason for its existence. A mission is constantly out there and worked toward, but never fully achieved. A good mission statement is broad and inspirational. It provides a destination to work toward.

Good brand mission statements:

- Reflect the authentic, personal, and differentiating values and motivations of the people inside the organization.
- Have strong emotional potential.
- Are consistently communicated throughout the organization.
- Are constantly reinforced at every opportunity.
- Allow some measurement to help determine progress and achievement.

Actual mission statements can take many different forms or structures. One good example of emotion, differentiation, and brevity from outside the technology industry is Saturn's very simple and straightforward aspiration to be "America's friendliest car company." Another good example is that of Steelcase: "Helping people work more effectively." Other strong brands, like Levi's, have three pages of aspiration, values, and mission to guide their brand-building efforts worldwide.

In the technology industry, several good examples of empowering brand mission statements exist. One is that of Gateway 2000, which describes both the company's vision and mission in its 1995 annual report:

"Our vision is to be the leading marketer of personal computer products in the world. We believe that means building a quality product at a competitive price. Our mission is to profitably grow our business faster than the competition by better understanding and serving the desires of our customers and aggressively marketing the highest value directly to our chosen markets."

Global Village Communications has the following statement of purpose:

"Our purpose is to make communications easy for personal computer users, whether it is fax, remote network access or access to information services. Our products will encourage the exchange of ideas and information between people, companies and countries."

The Claris mission is:

"To create and publish award-winning, simply powerful software to propel business, government, education and home users to even greater creativity and productivity."

All of these mission statements are broad and inspirational, and each, in its own unique way, provides a clear assertion of the company's purpose, which guides company direction and provides the brand with a foundation upon which to grow.

Brand Values and Culture

One of our contentions is that the role of the corporate brand is becoming more important for most technology companies. Many desirable and differentiating intangible brand attributes and values come from customers' feelings and perceptions about the company that makes the product. Also, as companies strive for every competitive advantage that they can muster – such as trying to achieve the lowest component costs or the most flexible product configurations – they are beginning to realize that, unlike product attributes, the one thing that competitors can't easily match is the uniqueness of the company itself. As we will discuss later, the overall brand experience plays an increasingly important role in differentiating brands. That's why corporate culture can be so important.

Products come and go. Technology changes. Market conditions evolve unexpectedly. But the culture and values of a brand can endure. Some companies, like Apple and Dell, start out with almost an intuitive sense of what their brand represents. Others have a culture that emerges, evolves, and even changes over time. Gateway, a company that cares a lot about values, has identified the following as the values its culture strives for and represents: respect, caring, teamwork, common sense, aggressiveness, honesty, efficiency, and fun. The company has changed and grown significantly in the past 10 years, but, as Gateway states in its 1995 annual report, "our values have remained the same." This type of consistency is very powerful and has a lot to do with Gateway's continuing growth and success.

As David Aaker points out: "The culture of an organization, more than procedures or structures, is ultimately what drives the attainment of sustainable advantage. Unless brand building becomes an organizational priority, it will be difficult for the organization to address difficult branding problems."[1]

This point is not about market positioning, but rather the core values, culture, and qualities of the brand. In other words, the things that guide all contacts with the customer and provide employees with direction and understanding for the day-to-day activities that contribute so much to a customer's perception of the brand. These qualities tend to be intangible values, like responsiveness and a commitment to innovation or reliability.

They are core, desirable values that the products and people of a company convey and deliver consistently over time.

As *Inc.* magazine reported in the November 1996 issue: "Companies with clever, highly evolved cultures have an advantage precisely because of the particular challenges of the current marketplace. Culture helps companies compete." Consider the impact of culture and values on brand building for a company like Hewlett Packard, where much of the brand strength comes from a culture –"The HP Way"– of responsiveness to customers, keeping promises, teamwork, and building high-quality, reliable products.

Here's how David Packard, co-founder of HP, views culture in his book *The HP Way*: "Any organization, any group of people who have worked together for some time, develops a philosophy, a set of values, a series of traditions and customs. These, in total, are unique to the organization... and guide us in meeting our objectives, in working with one another, and in dealing with customers, shareholders and others."[2]

Thus, companies with highly evolved cultures and broadly embraced values, like HP, have a powerful brand advantage because they can harness their uniqueness and power and make it part of the total brand experience. Without such a strong brand heritage, without a culture of teamwork and keeping promises, and without a reputation for building quality products, it's hard to imagine how the HP Pavilion home PCs could have entered the home market so late and become a top brand in less than a year (interestingly, the initial Pavilion launch campaign featured the tagline "It's not just a PC, it's an HP," a message which reflected the value connoted by the HP name alone). Likewise, while Sony entered the PC market even later than HP, it's no surprise that most observers expect Sony's brand power, which in part is derived from its innovation-oriented culture and ingrained brand values, to enable the company to deliver high-quality, differentiated product offerings and possibly succeed where many others have failed.

Commitment and Support

This third component to constructing a strong brand foundation means that companies must embrace and *commit* to brand building as a core business activity. This is where a company ties its brand mission to its company mission (if, in fact, the two are different) and fully commits to building the brand, just as it's fully committed to building the company. To do this effectively, top management needs to provide clear *support*, and adequate funding needs to be secured. This is critical to successful brand building. A brief look at some successful and less successful brands in the personal computer industry demonstrates the impact of top-management support on the success of both the brand and the company.

Apple's support for building a brand started with founder Steve Jobs and has continued under the tenures of John Scully, Michael Spindler, and Gilbert Amelio. Having long ago lost the platform war to Microsoft and Intel-based PCs, some argue that Apple could never have rebounded at all (as it did briefly in 1996) had it not been for the strength of its brand name. According to Carl Gustin, Chief Marketing Officer at Kodak and a former Apple marketing executive, "If they (Apple) weren't such a strong brand, they wouldn't have survived recent challenges. Apple's challenge is not a brand issue, it's a market standards issue."[3]

From their inception, two other leading personal computer brands, Dell and Gateway, have fortuitously had marketing-oriented CEOs who have not just supported investment in the brand, but insisted on it. As Mike Massaro, Chief Operating Officer at Goldberg Moser O'Neill, puts it: "Each of these two CEOs, Michael Dell and Ted Waitt, has set the pace, the attitude and the culture of their respective companies. And each has been a proponent of the brand. And it's not accidental that these two companies have had the most consistent communications in this industry for the past eight or nine years." It's no coincidence that they are also two of the strongest technology brands around today.

On the other hand, companies that have not invested sufficiently in their corporate brands due to an historical product-driven bias have suffered. At Novell, a company whose NetWare brand for many years was synonymous with "networking," the strength and high-recognition levels of the NetWare brand unfortunately have not translated to strength for the overall Novell brand because, historically, there was neither top-management nor financial support for long-term brand building.

Christine Hughes, former Senior Vice President of Corporate Marketing for Novell, describes the product-centric environment at

Novell this way: "When I arrived in December 1994, there were dozens of conflicting product names and a proliferation of subbrands – there was no systematic brand architecture in place... Budgets were held mostly in the various product groups, which each went their own way... Even after I was successful in convincing management to consolidate subbrands and agencies and launch a new corporate mark, the battles between the product groups and corporate marketing raged on, which, again, set back our important corporate branding initiatives."[4] And thus today, Novell is desperately trying to keep its NetWare franchise from losing more share to Windows NT and hoping to make up lost ground in the brand war against Microsoft, not an enviable challenge for any brand. While changing the name of the company's flagship product from NetWare to InternetWare is an admirable effort at repositioning for the new market reality, it is, in all likelihood, too late to regain the networking crown.

So, clearly, support for brand building means an enduring dedication to the cause, because a lack of support or even inconsistent support can result in an enduring competitive disadvantage.

In this chapter, we have presented the framework for *PowerBranding* and discussed how to go about establishing a strong brand foundation. In the next chapter, we will examine how to assess a brand, a key part of the brand management stage of *PowerBranding*.

4
Brand Assessment

To objectively see what consumers see is not easy.

– TIM AMBLER
Marketing From Advertising to Zen

Having lost sight of our objectives, we redoubled our efforts.

– OLD ADAGE

"What gets measured gets done" is one of the key tenets of the total quality management movement that has permeated numerous businesses throughout the world. From a quality perspective, this means that in order to continually improve the quality of your product you must establish a baseline of where it stands initially, then measure and track ongoing progress toward agreed-upon goals. Thus, the commitment to regular measurement itself serves as a catalyst to goal attainment.

This type of measurement and goal-setting approach can work equally well for technology marketers: in order to effectively guide and build your brand, you must first determine where it stands. But, as the opening quotes imply, brand assessment that properly measures customer perceptions is not necessarily an easy task, and mid-course branding adjustments are often driven by a "more is better" attitude that can result in putting emphasis in the wrong areas.

There are myriad ways to go about brand assessment, from simple focus-group explorations to the highly sophisticated financial and equity "scorecard" methods. This chapter will explore these and other unique approaches and examine some syndicated market measurements of brand status.

Financial Valuation

Probably the most sophisticated and controversial way to measure brand status is to utilize some form of financial analysis to arrive at a specific numerical valuation. The reason it's controversial is that there is presently no agreed-upon methodology or accounting rule to derive brand value. Plus, it's difficult to put an unassailable valuation of an intangible asset like a brand on a balance sheet. Nevertheless, many techniques are widely used to at least approximate brand value, especially to assist companies which acquire other companies and/or their brands.

In its ongoing survey of brand value, *Financial World* utilizes a hybrid formula comprised of two calculations to derive specific brand valuations. The magazine calculates the "earnings attributable" to a given brand on its own and relies on Interbrand's formula of these seven "multipliers" to calculate the "brand strength multiple:"[1]

- **Leadership**: brand's ability to influence its market.
- **Stability**: ability of the brand to survive.
- **Market**: strength of the brand's trading environment.
- **Internationality**: ability of the brand to cross geographic and cultural borders.
- **Trend**: direction of the brand's importance to its industry.
- **Support**: effectiveness of the brand's communications.
- **Protection**: brand owner's legal title.

In *Financial World's* August 1995 study, for example, Microsoft was deemed the "best-managed brand," with a brand value of $11.74 billion (exceeding its annual sales), while Apple was deemed one of the "most underutilized," with a brand value of only $1.35 billion (a fraction of its annual sales). In the magazine's April 1995 study, 19 software brands were evaluated, as shown in Figure 4-1.

Figure 4-1

Software Brand Rankings
Financial World, April 11, 1995

SOFTWARE BRAND	CURRENT VALUE (MIL.)	CHANGE IN VALUE FROM PRIOR YEAR	1994 SALES (MIL.)	1994 OPERATING INCOME (MIL.)
Microsoft	$10,287	570	4,449	1,049
IBM	3,748	216	11,346	1,676
Computer Associates	1,182	70	1,456	425
Oracle	931	113	1,130	305
Novell	628	-25	1,898	317
Adobe	276	18	598	103
Sybase	246	64	484	92
Corel	132	121	1164	45
Lotus	111	-57	942	14
Apple	103	65	190	31
Artisoft	38	-2	54	14
Delrina	25	D-P	101	27
Banyan	20	-37	119	3
Symantec	0	NA	265	19
Stac	0	P-D	26	-1
Software Publishing	0	NA	62	-10
Quarterdeck	0	P-D	27	-15
Borland	0	NA	392	-43
Intuit	0	NA	180	-132

A Diversity of Brand Assessment Techniques

While financial valuation is arguably the most elaborate approach to measuring brands, many other methods and techniques can also be used to evaluate a brand's status in the marketplace. One relatively simple way to take a quick pulse of the brand is by utilizing focus groups and/or telephone interviews to measure customer perceptions of the brand on key indicators of health and vitality, such as familiarity, likeability, and preference. Findings from such surveys can provide companies with useful insights on customer perceptions of the brand and can confirm whether intended messages are reaching their target audiences, if desirable attributes are associated with the brand, and, if so, to what degree.

A more sophisticated technique is represented by an Interbrand study that ranks the world's top brands on four criteria:

- **Weight**: the brand's market share within its category (35% of the total score).
- **Breadth**: how wide a slice of the world in terms of age, character, and nationality the brand speaks to (30% of the total score).
- **Depth**: loyalty of its customers (20% of the total score).
- **Length**: how far the brand can stretch beyond the original product type (15% of the total score).

Based on this evaluation, the world's top brands were deemed to be: McDonalds, Coca-Cola, Disney, Kodak, Sony, Gillette, Mercedes-Benz, Levi's, Microsoft, and Marlboro. Interestingly, as Microsoft continues to grow and develop its brand, the company is starting to appear at or near the top of the list in many brand evaluation studies that include non-technology categories.

BrandAsset Valuator™

A rather innovative approach to assessing brands is the Young & Rubicam BrandAsset Valuator, introduced in 1994. This approach is based on the assertion that brand strength has four components: *familiarity, relevance, esteem, and differentiation*. Based on a two-year study and interviews with 30,000 people in 19 countries covering 6,000 brands, this method plots where brand strength is today and where the brand could go in the future.

Although not focused on technology brands, this approach provides some stimulating thinking for technology brand managers. For example, familiarity and esteem combine to form a brand's *stature* in the marketplace. Relevance and differentiation combine to form a brand's *vitality*. Brands with high *stature* are usually the market leaders and biggest spenders, while brands that do best on *vitality* are characterized more by the quality of the ideas and creativity surrounding their brand-building efforts. Some top brands, like Coca-Cola, Sony, and Mercedes-Benz, are among the leaders in both categories. Others, known for their flair and strong emotional appeal, like Nike, Disney, and Porsche, rise to the top of the vitality list. Y&R tends to believe that *vitality* is also a key indicator of growth potential (although not in all cases, as Porsche demonstrates, for example).

Top 10 brands from Y&R BrandAsset Valuator (1994):

Stature	Vitality
1. Coca-Cola	1. Coca-Cola
2. Kodak	2. Nike
3. Sony	3. Adidas
4. Mercedes-Benz	4. Sony
5. Pepsi-Cola	5. Ferrari
6. Nestle	6. Reebok
7. Gillette	7. Disney
8. Colgate	8. Porsche
9. Adidas	9. Pepsi-Cola
10. Volkswagen	10. Mercedes-Benz

What's interesting about the Y&R approach is that it affirms that brand building really starts with differentiation and the unique position a brand occupies in the customer's mind.

Communications Audit

Some companies approach brand assessment primarily from a communications perspective and conduct what is commonly referred to as a communications audit. The first step in this process involves gathering and examining representative samples of all communications materials that a company produces, such as advertising, brochures, business papers, electronic media (e.g. CD-ROM, Web site), newsletters, packaging, press releases, signage, and technical bulletins.

The next step is to carefully analyze all of the communications materials and observe the totality of the brand as communicated to the outside world from the customer's perspective. Is a uniform image being communicated or are several conflicting images and messages being sent from what appears to be different companies, rather than a single company? If the latter is true, what should be done about it?

This type of basic audit can provide useful insights into brand status. To examine brand communications even further, however, it's also helpful to review them with at least four criteria in mind:

- **Consistency**, in terms of brand identity – the look and feel and tonality; and in terms of messaging – the consistent use of key messages throughout various communications.
- **Quality**, both in the clarity of communications and in the strength of creative executions.
- **Integration** of messages across a variety of different communications and across different communications channels.
- **Results**, in terms of measurement of effectiveness of communications and goal achievement.

This process of developing a broad, clear perspective on the total communications landscape can thus serve as the foundation for establishing future goals to improve communications and communications effectiveness. Yet, while a communications audit is a good place to start for many companies, it is often done in a very subjective manner that does not typically provide the kind of insights necessary to effectively guide company efforts toward building stronger brands. Also, it can sometimes just lead to different, not better, communications.

Market Measurements of Brand Status

In addition to measuring one's brand status via an overall communications audit, many market measurements are available today, some widely published and others only on a subscription basis, to assist technology companies in evaluating the status of their brand(s).

As mentioned earlier, IDG's research on the purchase process for information technology products provides the technology companies surveyed with a lot of comparative data on the relative strength of their brands. These studies include a variety of assessments on how different companies are perceived and which attributes they are most closely associated with by the research participants.

For example, in Wave VI, *Brand and the Buying Process*, the percentage of business respondents who associated a given brand with "reliability" varied greatly, as shown in Figure 4-2. Perceived reliability is known to be a key factor that influences brand preference and strength. Therefore, companies which scored poorly on this measurement are alerted to the need to address their perceived shortcomings.

Another brand assessment example is a type of measurement that helps companies better understand their perceived brand personalities. Also from Wave VI, Figure 4-3 provides a composite perspective of the HP brand personality by showing how HP rated against 16 other hardware manufacturers on 10 personality-related attributes. HP was seen as a "trustworthy" company that "cares about what customers think." It was not perceived to be as "friendly" or as "cool/hip" as other brands.

Figure 4-2

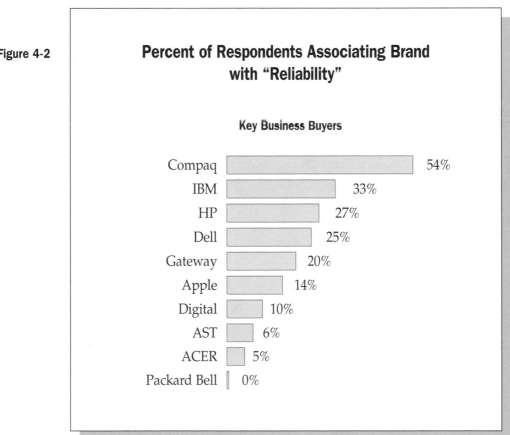

Percent of Respondents Associating Brand with "Reliability"

Key Business Buyers

Compaq	54%
IBM	33%
HP	27%
Dell	25%
Gateway	20%
Apple	14%
Digital	10%
AST	6%
ACER	5%
Packard Bell	0%

Figure 4-3

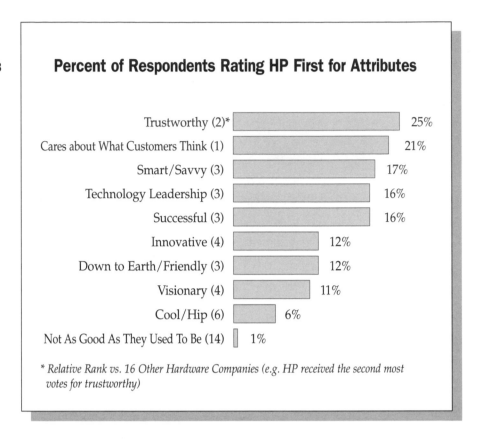

Percent of Respondents Rating HP First for Attributes

Trustworthy (2)* — 25%
Cares about What Customers Think (1) — 21%
Smart/Savvy (3) — 17%
Technology Leadership (3) — 16%
Successful (3) — 16%
Innovative (4) — 12%
Down to Earth/Friendly (3) — 12%
Visionary (4) — 11%
Cool/Hip (6) — 6%
Not As Good As They Used To Be (14) — 1%

* Relative Rank vs. 16 Other Hardware Companies (e.g. HP received the second most votes for trustworthy)

Other approaches to brand assessment are available from IntelliQuest and provide ongoing measurements of brand status for technology products. One of the more widely used measurements is Intellitrack IQ™, a sophisticated family of continuous tracking studies covering desktop, portable, printer, and networking products. These measure brand awareness, consideration, loyalty, image (perceptions), and reasons for won/lost business.

This type of assessment is useful in measuring the impact of communications programs and various marketing activities in addition to the overall status of the brand. As shown is Figure 4-4, IDG's Wave V research found that there is a near-perfect correlation between awareness of a brand and consideration for that brand. This correlation can also be seen as a two-to-one relationship – that is, a company's unaided awareness percentage is approximately twice as much as its consideration percentage. Companies that show greater than a two-to-one relationship between awareness and consideration, as IBM does in Figure 4-4, are thus alerted to potential comparative inefficiencies in their communications and/or demand creation programs.

Figure 4-4

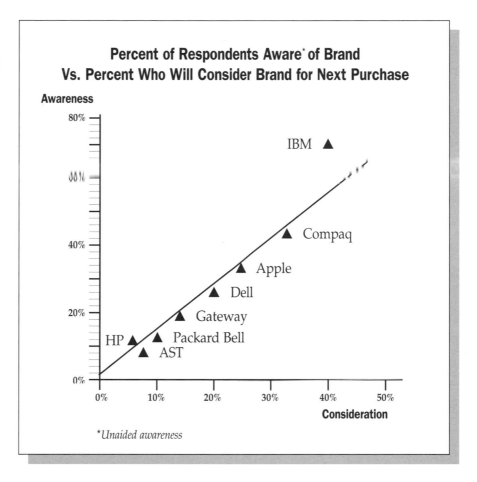

**Percent of Respondents Aware* of Brand
Vs. Percent Who Will Consider Brand for Next Purchase**

*Unaided awareness

Another comprehensive brand assessment tool is available from Techtel Corporation, a marketing research and consulting firm. The Techtel Demand Management System provides technology marketers with key measures of market demand, such as awareness, consideration, and opinion.

As the example in Figure 4-5 shows, Dell experienced a dramatic drop and subsequent recovery in "positive opinion," as well as "repeat consideration" for its notebook products. Positive opinion about Dell notebooks began to drop early in 1993, well before Dell publicly announced that an earnings drop (on May 26, 1993) was related to its notebook-line problems. By the second quarter of 1996, positive opinion for Dell notebooks had almost recovered to pre-drop levels, with repeat consideration recovering and even surpassing pre-drop levels. These types of measurements provide marketers with a means to gauge their

Figure 4-5

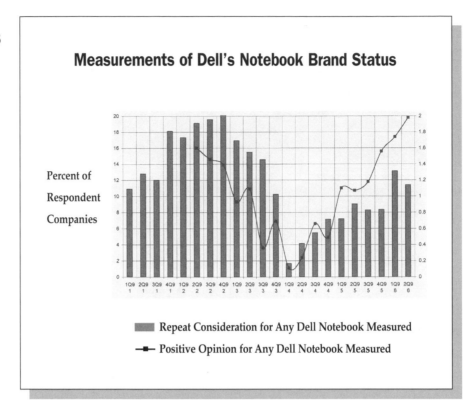

Measurements of Dell's Notebook Brand Status

Percent of Respondent Companies

■ Repeat Consideration for Any Dell Notebook Measured

─■─ Positive Opinion for Any Dell Notebook Measured

brand status in the marketplace, as well as provide insight into brand strength dimensions, like positive opinion and repeat consideration, that can also serve as "leading indicators" of business performance.

In this chapter, we have explored various ways for determining how your brand is currently doing in the marketplace – from a brand-strength perspective. In the final analysis, however, the exact methodology used to conduct brand assessment is not necessarily as important as ensuring that ongoing measurement is taking place. In technology markets, one could argue that it's even more important to regularly monitor brand status than in less dynamic markets – primarily because the rapid pace of technological change and product obsolescence can result in more frequent changes in brand status. This fact has led us to develop a technique that enables companies to diagnose the "fitness" of their brands on a regular basis, which we shall explore in the next chapter.

5

BrandFitness™

Every brand faces unique marketplace challenges. Threats come from both outside the company, in the form of competitors who have your brand in their "crosshairs," and from inside the company. Often the inside threats – battles for budget control, consistency, and creative autonomy; short-term thinking; lack of process and discipline; and a myopic focus on deliverables – can be just as daunting as the outside ones. But unless companies know where the weaknesses and vulnerabilities of their brands lie, they can't take the proper corrective actions to strengthen their brands.

Some of the assessment techniques discussed in the prior chapter, like valuation, give companies a high-level or "macro" view of their brand's situation and status. Other approaches, such as IntelliQuest's or Techtel's tracking services, can provide useful trend-line views that help companies keep brand development on track and alert them to take corrective action if and when brand development starts to fall off track. But while each of these approaches is useful, none of them totally uncovers the status of a brand.

This is why we developed *BrandFitness*, a practical, comprehensive approach to brand assessment that can help individuals involved in managing brands better understand the current condition of their brands and gain important insights into how to best improve them. Brands, like people, can get flabby and out of shape, or remain underdeveloped unless they follow a good fitness regimen. Since a good fitness regime should always start with a thorough check-up, we have outlined the most important considerations for fully diagnosing your brand's health and vitality.

BrandFitness™ Audit and Assessment Methodology

The five steps to a complete *BrandFitness* assessment include:

- Determination of company goals and objectives for the brand(s).
- Identification and understanding of the internal corporate realities that affect the ability of the company to manage brands successfully.
- Compilation, integration, and analysis of current customer knowledge and competitive information.
- Diagnostics of both internal and external customer knowledge and marketplace information, with corporate brand-building objectives and goals in mind.
- Recommendations (prescription) for actions.

Following is a detailed discussion of each of these steps.

Step 1: Determination of Company Goals and Objectives for the Brand(s)

The first step is to determine the corporate goals and objectives for the brand(s), both in terms of short-term sales support and long-term marketing and corporate goals. Here, one should also probe to determine what leverage and competitive advantages are desired from building brand equity.

This step includes identification of brands and markets to assess key market segments, competition, target customer profiles and priorities, key issues, historical data, and other relevant marketplace, product, and distribution information.

Step 2: Identification and Analysis of Internal Realities

This step primarily consists of interviews with appropriate senior management, marketing, sales, and product management personnel, as well as key partners, like advertising and PR agencies and dedicated suppliers. Focus-group discussions with employees from different regions and parts of the company are often helpful here, too. The following key areas are typically probed:

Management

Assess senior and marketing management's understanding and support of, as well as commitment to, brand building – plus their views on key issues.

Organization
Analyze internal structure, responsibilities, and dependencies that help/ hinder brand-building efforts and directly impact resolution of brand issues and achievement of brand goals. Also, look at the international organization as it impacts global brand building.

Products
Review product and technology information, including segmentation and distribution plans.

Planning process
Take a broad look at the communications planning policies and procedures currently in place and/or necessary to implement effective, integrated brand-building programs. Also, look at communications effectiveness and accountability. Finally, gather information about the current level of customer (and target prospect) knowledge and the process for obtaining ongoing feedback.

Perceptions and attitudes
Examine the internal views of brand assets and liabilities, internal and external obstacles and hurdles to overcome, customer perception of the brand, etc.

Brand and corporate identity
Review key elements of the existing brand-identity and corporate-identity programs (name, design, tonality), product naming conventions, trademark protection, etc.

Other proprietary assets
Examine any appropriate and leveragable brand-building assets, such as corporate equity, patents, technology, alliances, distribution, key employees, etc.

Step 3: Compilation and Review of External Perceptions and Beliefs
This step is a review of customer and prospect perceptions, beliefs, and attitudes relating to corporate and product brands. The input may

also include feedback from other brand influencers (e.g. media and analysts). You can collect this information primarily through review of existing research but may also need to interview a limited number of key customers and purchase influencers. Important brand dimensions to examine are:

Awareness and familiarity

Levels of aided and unaided awareness, overall and by key market segments. Familiarity and consideration. Comparisons to key competitors are important.

Image and positioning

Brand associations and attributes, personality and perceptions of competitive differentiation.

Preference

Quality, value, and price/value perceptions, attribute importance, intent to buy versus the competition – by all key target market segments.

Distribution

Review of channel strengths and weaknesses. Competitive comparisons are important here. What is the basis for brand equity with the channel: is it price, quality, market niche, responsiveness, or something else?

Loyalty

Customer satisfaction/dissatisfaction, loyalty by segments, repeat purchase intention, win/lose versus the competition. Also, a look at customer retention programs and customer accessibility.

NOTE: This step makes extensive use of existing research and information that the company already has or can get quickly from outside resources. In some cases, research to get important customer intelligence that is not current or is missing is recommended.

Step 4: Diagnostics

After gathering the information from steps 2 and 3, analyze it in the context of key marketing and business issues, goals, and specific objectives of the assessment project. Be sure to take a customer-centric rather than product-centric approach to problem and opportunity resolution. Gaps in knowledge are identified here, and a summary of brand strengths and weaknesses is also provided.

Step 5: Recommendations for Actions

Specific, recommended actions are identified and prioritized along with action plans for resolving issues, developing new policies and procedures, etc. These recommendations become the foundation for the strategic and prescriptive direction to meet the company's brand-building goals identified and agreed to earlier. Recommended actions also include determination of appropriate brand-equity metrics and measurements. These recommendations, including appropriate documentation, are then presented to the individual(s) responsible for initiating the audit and other interested management personnel.

A thorough brand audit or assessment that follows this structure will take about four to eight weeks to complete. It can be done internally and is often an ideal task-force project. The danger of doing this job solely using internal resources, however, is that it lacks true objectivity. For that reason, it can make sense to engage outside consultants who are skilled at this sort of analysis and measurement technique.

If, on the other hand, a company lacks the time or the resources to undertake a comprehensive audit as described, the next section presents an alternative approach we developed for conducting a "self diagnosis" — i.e. one that can be easily and quickly accomplished by internal company participants.

BrandFitness™: Short-Form Checklist and Examination

This approach to brand assessment is a self-diagnostic tool that enables technology companies to make a fairly quick assessment of the health of their brands. The scoring and findings of this brand check-up allow companies to better understand the overall health of brands and use this knowledge to devise more effective brand-building strategies and programs.

The following checklist (and discussion points) is clearly not meant as a way to evaluate product functions or features. It's meant to focus on things that can influence the more intangible dimensions and values of the product – those things that generally come along with brand name and reputation. This process can also be used to uncover and articulate the goals that new brands should strive to achieve. In conducting this examination, we advise companies to think about each statement in terms of where the brand stands today – then check the most appropriate response. A guide to scoring responses is found at the end of the checklist.

BrandFitness™ Short-Form Checklist

1. **Clear statement of overall brand purpose and direction:**

Yes	❏ 0
Not yet	❏ 2

   Discussion
   What business are you in?
   What does the brand now stand for in the marketplace?
   Where do you see the brand in two to five years?
   What's unique about the brand?

2. **Brand culture and values known and supported:**

Yes	❏ 0
More intuitive	❏ 1
Not really	❏ 2

   Discussion
   What qualities or characteristics seem to be enduring about
      the brand?
   Have these changed over time?
   How do customers perceive the brand's values?
   Are brand culture and company culture aligned?

3. **Top management support of brand-building efforts:**

Strong	❏ 0
Adequate	❏ 2
Pretty shaky/no	❏ 4

   Discussion
   For top management:
      What does brand mean to you?
      How important is brand?
      What brands do you admire and why?
      What is your company doing today to build the brand?

For others:

> How much does top management understand about brand building?
> How supportive are they of these efforts? Provide recent examples.

4. Internal brand champion:

Strong champion with authority	❑ 0
A champion with the responsibility	❑ 1
Not at a level to make a real difference	❑ 3

Discussion
In the organization, who is the highest ranking person you could call a
    brand champion?
Is brand management responsibility fragmented or consolidated?

5. Internal planning policies and procedures:

Strategic and disciplined	❑ 0
Pretty strong	❑ 1
Need some improvement	❑ 2
Pretty much ad hoc, tactical	❑ 3

Discussion
Tell us about your marketing, advertising, and communications
planning process:
> Who has budget control?
> How are budgets established?
> Who has review and approval authority?

6. Would you describe your company as:

Customer-driven	❑ 0
Technology-driven	❑ 1
Sales/profit-driven	❑ ?
Competitor-driven	❑ 3

Discussion
How would you describe the company?
How would customers?
Why do you say that?

7. Does your company consider brand building as:

A core business function	❑ 0
Virtually synonymous with marketing	❑ 1
Primarily a marcom responsibility	❑ 3

Discussion
How systematic is your company's approach to brand management?
Is brand a consideration in nearly every business decision?

8. **Integration of communications plans:**

Planning done jointly and strategically	❏ 0
Coordinated but not well integrated	❏ 1
Not done, needs much improvement	❏ 3

Discussion
Tell us about your communications planning process:
    How well integrated are your programs across different channels
        of communication?
    Is database marketing done well?
    Who drives the integration planning process?
    What are some examples of integrated communications?

9. **Long-term brand identity strategy:**

Clear, comprehensive plan in place	❏ 0
Identity guidelines exist	❏ 2
Not yet	❏ 4

Discussion
Tell us/show us the brand identity strategy:
    Does it include personality?
    Show us the materials prepared in different places.

10. **Brand-naming convention:**

Simple and well-documented	❏ 0
Can generally keep things under control	❏ 1
Product managers still come up with names	❏ 3

Discussion
Tell us/show us the brand-naming strategy:
    How well is it working?

11. **Number of product brands to support/manage:**

Limited number, well defined	❏ 0
Getting to be too many to handle well	❏ 2
Way too confusing, need to cut back	❏ 4

Discussion
How many different product brands do you have today?
How many a year ago?
How are they different?
Is that difference meaningful to the marketplace?
What is the budget behind each product brand?
What new products are coming up?

12. **Product/brand segmentation strategy:**

Very tight and well-defined approach	❑ 0
Overly fragmented, too many	❑ 2
Doesn't exist, we'll sell to anybody	❑ 3

Discussion
How are your product brands segmented?
What research supports that approach?
How well is it working?

13. **Marketing support and communications budget:**

Enough to do the job	❑ -2
Not as much as we'd like	❑ 0
It comes and goes	❑ 2
Severely underfunded to do the job	❑ 4

Discussion
Review budget for communications activities:
　　How is budget established?
　　What was it last year?
　　What will it be next year?
　　How does it compare to that of the competition?

14. **Advertising support:**

Consistent, strategic, distinctive, and high quality	❑ 0
Good ads but lacks consistent funding	❑ 1
Inconsistent, tactical, feature-focused	❑ 3

Discussion
Review advertising programs:
　　What are the opinions inside the company?
　　What are the opinions of the ad agency?

15. **Marketing communications ROI:**

We have a very good idea of what we get back from our marcom investments	❑ 0
Periodically we measure results	❑ 1
I wish we knew	❑ 3

Discussion
What kind of tracking or measurement is done for specific programs?
Is funding adequate?

16. **Attention to details:**

No brand-building detail is too small	❏ 0
We know we should be doing better	❏ 1
Come on, who has the time?	❏ 2

Discussion

How consistently are little things done to support the brand-building efforts

Is there a common look and feel to all printed material?

Are brand guidelines provided for sales, support, and other customer contact people?

17. **Knowledge of customer:**

Constant and current feedback in place	❏ 0
Adequate research done recently	❏ 1
We really should be doing more	❏ 3

Discussion

Review research about customers:
  How well is it linked to areas like customer satisfaction and field sales support?
  Is information summarized and distributed broadly?

18. **Committed, profitable customers:**

Strong loyalty, repurchase rates known	❏ 0
We're competitive enough	❏ 1
Who really knows?	❏ 3

Discussion

How much of the business today comes from repeat customers?

How do you know the degree of your customer commitment versus that of the competition?

How much is a customer worth over the expected "customer life cycle"?

What is being done to target more profitable customers?

19. **Post-purchase relationship building:**

Strong and consistent reinforcement,on a personal basis	❏ 0
Periodic programs to target and/or acknowledge good customers	❏ 1
They bought once, they'll buy again	❏ 3

Discussion

Is there a useful, comprehensive customer database?

What programs and communications target the customer base?

What's the budget for this?

20. **Multi-national branding:**

Consistent, shared values and messages, localized as appropriate	❏ 0
Common goals but fairly autonomous	❏ 1
The countries go their own ways	❏ 3

Discussion
How do you communicate brands globally?
Who controls the budget?
How often do the geographies talk and get together?

21. **Multi-national brand planning:**

Constant, close communication and country involvement	❏ 0
We talk but could do better	❏ 1
Corporate issues direction and funding	❏ 3

Discussion
Is there real-time dissemination of communications messages and materials?
What is the global planning process for brand advertising and other communications?

22. **Awareness:**

High, unaided awareness in key markets	❏ 0
Okay, but could be better	❏ 1
Not at competitive levels, needs boost	❏ 3

Discussion
How does your awareness (especially unaided) compare to that of the competition by key market segment?
How current is the information?
When will the data be gathered again?

23. **Quality perceptions:**

We know we're right up there with the best	❏ 0
We think we're doing okay	❏ 1
Not one of our strengths, unfortunately	❏ 4

Discussion
What data is there on quality perceptions?
What does quality mean to the customer?

24. Familiarity:

Most people in our target know us well	❏ 0
It's getting better	❏ 1
Way below what it should be	❏ 3

Discussion
What do you know about the depth of familiarity for the brand –
    and about how it compares to that of your competition?
Do you have a consistent definition of familiarity?

25. Likeability:

Most people enjoy doing business with us	❏ 0
We're doing better than before	❏ 1
Who cares if they like us or not	❏ 3

Discussion
What, if any, measures exist on this beyond anecdotal evidence?
How does it compare to that of competition?

26. Image and personality:

We have a desirable, distinctive image	❏ 0
Image could be in tighter focus	❏ 1
Not as clear or well defined as it could be	❏ 3

Discussion
Review of current research should answer this.

27. Associations attached to the brand:

Strong, motivating, and differentiating	❏ 0
Weak, could be more motivating and differentiating	❏ 1
None of the above	❏ 3
Strong and differentiating but not motivating	❏ 4

Discussion
Review of current research should answer this.

28. Availability to customers:

Easily and widely available at most times	❏ 0
Distribution could always be better	❏ 1
Not widely available, often late or on allocation	❏ 3

Discussion
Here, review your distribution process and channel relationships.
What has changed or is changing?

29. Accessibility to customers:

Highly accessible and responsive	❏ 0
We're improving all the time	❏ 1
Not a strong point for us, yet	❏ 3

Discussion
What things are you doing to build a relationship with customers?
How is it working?

How Fit Is Your Brand?

Total up the score for each question. If multiple people are taking the checkup, tally the scores and use the average to determine where your brand or brands fall in the "fitness range." Be aware, however, that it's not really the score that's most helpful here; it's looking at the individual responses to each question and determining the most pressing issues and priority actions to take. No individual or brand can get in shape overnight. True fitness comes from a focus on the kind of brand-influencing activities and actions that you can isolate and strengthen through consistent and conscientious work on an ongoing basis.

Fitness Range:

0 - 19	Top shape, ready to go the distance – not much room for improvement.
20 - 34	Admirable performance – but could use more regular workouts.
35 - 49	Just getting by, too soft – need to develop a more disciplined regimen.
50 +	Flabby, weak brand – major fitness overhaul needed.

Ultimately, whether a company uses one or more of the approaches to brand assessment that we discussed in Chapter 4 or the *BrandFitness* approaches examined in this chapter, brand assessment is basically a part, albeit a very significant one, of the entire brand-management process. As we shall explore further in the next chapter, while understanding the health of your brand is important, managing your brand effectively is critical.

6
Brand Management

Brand management stands at the junction of company and customer, and it must integrate the totally different decision dynamics of the two worlds.

– DAVID ARNOLD,
The Handbook of Brand Management

Brands are the real capital of business, yet brand management is still in its infancy.

– JEAN-NOEL KAPFERER,
Strategic Brand Management

As we discussed in Chapter 1, many things get in the way of successful branding at technology companies. Sometimes, it's a lack of understanding that brands can have a tremendous influence on the success of one company versus another. Other times, it's the blinding focus on getting products to market and having to deliver new releases faster than ever, i.e. in "Internet time"– a phrase coined to describe how the Internet has compressed development cycles and compelled companies to accomplish everything in less time.

David Arnold's remark about the differing dynamics of the *internal* company and the *external* customer alludes to the challenge of reconciling company requirements with customer requirements. Inside a company, especially a public one, there is relentless day-to-day pressure to dedicate effort and resources to meet short-term objectives, to deliver immediate results, and to "make the quarter." While on the outside, customers are more concerned about the longer-term aspects of technology purchases, about product obsolescence, about the total cost of ownership, and about whether they are investing in the right solution, the right brand, and the right company – for both now and the future.

Effectively balancing these two different worlds is what brand management is all about. Finding a way to cope with the pressing internal requirements to generate sales, while remaining focused on achieving the long-term goal of building a strong brand and increasing brand equity. Brand management is not an easy task in any industry, but it's certainly more difficult to do in an industry that is more interrupt-driven than methodical and characterized more by continual change than constancy.

In this chapter, we will take a look at brand management *and* brand building from a systems standpoint *and* a structural one, because without both – without well-defined processes to manage brands *and* without adequate human and financial resources to build brands – it's difficult to succeed. We will also examine a variety of brand-management challenges and explore an integrated approach to thinking about brand management that fosters branding at a more strategic level.

Building and Managing Technology Brands

Although brand management is a formidable challenge, it's nevertheless doable. While it requires patience, dedication, and discipline, it's all about having the appropriate systems, structure, and process to guide the effective management of brands on a daily basis and over the long haul. There are almost as many ways to go about managing brands as there are companies that seek to manage them, yet, from our experience and observations, the most powerful method is to develop and install a comprehensive brand-management system at the very core of a business, just as one would install a microprocessor and an operating system at the core of a personal computer.

We believe that smart brand management starts with a clear understanding of what *brand building* is all about. Brand building is not about running some new ads, developing a new logo, or coming up with a snappy, new tag line. Those things may be, and often are, part of a brand-building effort, but effective brand building is more fundamental and far more complex. We define it this way:

Brand building is the systematic *process* **of understanding and managing the perceptions and experiences customers associate with a brand in a manner that creates added value and preference over competitive alternatives.**

While this may sound like an overly academic definition, it contains some very important implications for managing brands. First, brand building is a *process*, not an event. Too many technology companies still believe that image or corporate advertising campaigns and splashy product launches, combined with good press, are the best ways to build brands. While successful brands are certainly supported by those activities, it takes much more. It takes an orchestration of many communications and marketing activities, consistently integrated over time, to build a winning brand. To ensure success, brand building and brand management must be based on a broader, more continuous, longer-term view.

Unless you understand current *customer perceptions* (and the quality of customer brand experiences) based on objective feedback from a variety of sources, you can't manage brands to your advantage. To acquire this understanding, it's necessary to go beyond the typical quarterly tracking information often used in brand management and regularly engage in direct interaction with customers – on the phone, on the Internet, in the lab, etc. – so the feedback is timely and based on a more diverse and representative sample of customers.

In addition, managing *customer experiences* means having the capability to influence those parts of the organization that touch customers. Every contact with a customer can either help or hurt brand-building efforts. For example, even how a company handles on-hold phone waits can have an influence on brand perceptions, especially if one wants to be seen as a responsive or caring brand. Effective brand management depends on a supportive organization which sees almost every customer-related issue or program in a brand context. And it requires adequate structure and resources to succeed.

Finally, creating *added value* is ultimately every brand manager's goal. Added value can naturally take many forms. For Gateway, it's not just a good price; it's also friendly, caring people. For Yahoo, it's not just great search capability; it's an inviting attitude of fun and youthfulness. Of course, added value resides in the customer's perception of a real difference. Because, if a company's *added value* is not recognized or valued and it doesn't create or sustain preference over the competition, it is really not of *value* and, therefore, offers no advantage. It may, in fact, merely increase costs.

Guidelines for Brand Building and Brand Management

Brand building is only as powerful as an organization allows it to be. A supportive organization that makes proactive efforts to do the things that foster brand building is critical. If building and managing a brand or family of brands is desirable, then how can technology companies make the internal adjustments and take the actions necessary to increase their chances for long-term brand success? There is no single "one size fits all" formula that is appropriate for this industry. The category and individual company challenges are far too dynamic. But there are some sensible guidelines that can help all companies. A successful brand-building and management system is characterized by what we call the "Six C's"– basic principles that guide brand development and management and enhance brand sensitivity in an organization:

- **Customer** focus, right from the start of planning.
- **Champions** of the brand, with responsibility and authority.
- **Capability**, in terms of organization and resources.
- **Common** practices and policies.
- **Consciousness** of brand issues guiding everyday activities.
- **Consistency** of messages, processes, methods, and experiences with the brand.

Customer Focus

What does it mean to be customer focused? It means that successful brand management starts and ends with the customer, not with the product. Intuit is a good example of a company which has built winning brands like Quicken, because the company's founder, Scott Cook, possesses a strong and unwavering commitment to be customer focused. Marketing managers at Intuit believe that the company's key competitive difference is in its partnership with customers, which includes constant, direct customer contact with engineering and product development. "It's a key part of the company philosophy – and competitive advantage – to involve the customer in everything we do," says Jacqueline Marteense, Group Marketing Manager for Quicken.

As discussed earlier, this principle of customer focus is key to brand success. If an organization is fundamentally more technology or competitor driven, it will be difficult to make real progress in aligning all areas for building strong brands.

Champions of the Brand

Technology companies also need empowered brand champions at different levels. The CEO, of course, needs to be the top corporate brand champion. Andy Grove was initially skeptical of the "Intel Inside" brand-building effort, but he took a calculated leap of faith. Early results convinced him that it was worth the effort and investment, and now he's the staunchest brand supporter at Intel. Lou Gerstner at IBM comes from industries where brand building and savvy brand-management practices have been institutionalized. His belief that the IBM brand provides strong competitive advantages shows up in the smart ways IBM has revitalized its corporate brand and various subbrands. At Microsoft, the brand champion is COO Bob Herbold, formerly with Proctor and Gamble. His role is to bring discipline and clarity to the brand-building process. Even smaller and newer companies like Knowledge Adventure and Yahoo have founders who recognize and champion the efforts to create brand differentiation in big and little ways.

Companies likewise need brand champions looking after individual brands. Product managers have traditionally focused on marketing tasks centered around developing products, forging alliances, securing distribution, coordinating with sales, and overseeing other product-centric tasks. Few product managers have the word "brand" in their job description, yet more should. As companies begin to recognize that the bigger challenge today is not just selling *product* but also getting customers to buy into a *brand*, they need to redefine the scope of product management. Some companies have already moved to a brand management-oriented – as opposed to product management-oriented – structure. This approach creates the formal responsibility and authority for brand managers to deal more effectively with the complexities of brand building. Other companies have retained structures where product managers remain primarily focused on traditional *product* development activities – but have added brand managers to assume responsibility for all *brand* development activities.

A more radical idea, one that's emerging in other industries, is the position of a brand-equity manager. Tom Peters has even suggested that any company with more than $250 million in sales should have a vice president for brand equity. Ideally, this would be a senior-level person with both the responsibility and authority to guide, monitor, and change brand-building programs anywhere in the organization.

Other companies have turned to brand task forces and brand-equity committees in an effort to champion brand building inside the organization. For example, National Semiconductor's committee of representatives from six different parts of the organization meets regularly to consider brand-related issues. The risk, however, is that task forces and committees lack any real authority to implement consistent brand-building practices and policies throughout the organization and often lead to ineffective implementation of recommendations.

One inadvisable approach is having the advertising or PR agency assume the role of brand champion for a company. While agencies certainly know a lot about building brands, most, unfortunately, come to the planning table with limited access to the broad range of communications options necessary to build brands. More importantly, however, if brand building is seen as something initiated by the agency, the company will not embrace the idea as thoroughly or fundamentally as it must to get on with the job. Good agencies certainly can and ought to be allies in preparing and selling through brand-building programs, but companies need to take ownership themselves and have brand champions who drive the organization from the inside.

Capability

Capability refers to an organization's willingness and ability to manage brands effectively. It means having the right organizational structure, charters, and resources to proactively manage brands. It's not enough to have brand champions and common practices if the organization itself creates insurmountable barriers to effective brand building. Companies need to move away from compartmentalized thinking about brand management and the constraining belief that it's only the responsibility of a brand, marcom, or product manager.

Brand building is not even solely a marketing function. Brand building, like total quality management, needs to be seen as a core business requirement and a part of everybody's responsibility. Companies need to embrace brand building on a horizontal, cross-functional basis. It can no longer be viewed as a specialist function. Therefore, product and brand managers need new skills for managing cross-functionally. Managing strategy, ambiguity, contention, and indirect reports becomes critical to success.

Ironically, technology companies, especially start-ups, may have some inherent advantages from an organizational viewpoint to accomplish this. Unlike tradition-bound organizations in other industries, technology companies are generally leaner and flatter and potentially able to respond more quickly to change. They are also more accustomed to cross-functional planning for activities like product development and new product introductions. On the other hand, constant reorganizations typical in the technology industry may serve to offset the aforementioned advantages.

Common Practices and Policies

Common practices and policies are another important characteristic of successful brand-management systems. Many companies which are conscious of brand importance, have, nevertheless, overlooked the need to train people in applying disciplined approaches to important branding practices like naming, advertising development, corporate identity, customer and market segmentation, research, and new brand introductions. This is a particular problem for technology companies that are highly decentralized. Field and/or channel people often have budget responsibility for local or cooperative promotion efforts, working with local or specialist agencies. While these may not be high-impact brand activities, everything counts. Often we have also seen briefing documents – and the skills applied in developing them – vary widely across and among divisions of a single company. That's why every company should have a single, standard method or format for briefing advertising and other communications firms at the front end when developing any new campaign or program.

Naming is another important area where companies need to apply more common practices and policies. Product and brand managers should have guidelines for not only developing new names in a disciplined manner but also determining when new names are warranted.

Consciousness

Higher consciousness of brand issues results when an organization has a goal to educate and evangelize brand importance throughout the entire company. Successfully managing a brand requires a lot of education about what a brand is, why it is important, and how it should be managed on a day-to-day basis. To do this effectively, companies must ensure that the language of branding is broadly understood. Without the proper terminology or branding language, you can't communicate – you can't instill "understanding" and build consensus about what needs to be done. Nearly every manager in a technology company understands that software bugs or hardware failures can cause product schedules to slip – these are standard product development terms. But not all understand even basic branding terms – or that the failure to properly build and manage a brand can make even the best-engineered product fall short of success.

It's important, then, to commit to educating and raising the consciousness of employees, so that individuals at every level understand why brand makes a difference and what their roles and responsibility are. That way, you'll ensure that they are contributing to building the brand. At Microsoft, Greg Perlot, former Director of Worldwide Advertising, found it took more time than expected to build appreciation for brand building inside the company: "There is a sensitivity and respect now about the value of the Microsoft brand that didn't exist two years ago. Our people understand that having the Microsoft name on your product gives it a better chance of selling than not – and we have incontrovertible data to back this up." IBM, as another example, has done a good job of internal education throughout the company, so all employees are on board with the brand-building efforts and all contribute wherever possible. Finally, as Christine Hughes, who led corporate marketing for Novell for a couple of years, learned when introducing an important new logo and tagline, "You can't *over-communicate* (with employees) about the brand-building changes you're making." It's critical to brand building, then, to make strong and consistent internal communications and education a priority.

Consistency

Consistency is the driver of powerful brands. Winning brands are characterized by consistency of messages – what they say to customers and how they say it. Whether by intention or by process of elimination, strong brands select a few key messages and consistently deliver them across all communications. Strong brands are also characterized by consistency of tone and attitude. They don't change personality with every new advertising campaign or new product launch. Consistency of tone and attitude allows customers to become familiar with a brand on an emotional basis, as they might with a person. Consider Gateway's distinct brand personality and how consistently the company has stuck with a "cow-spotted" tone and manner – on everything from advertisements to catalogs to the web site.

Ultimately, powerful brands are distinguished by a consistent presence in the marketplace. For example, consistency in advertising is very important. Too many companies fail to appreciate the impact of maintaining a presence through consistent advertising, especially to key audiences. They start and stop campaigns and initiatives almost every quarter. This constant communications churning only serves to confuse customers, who remain unsure of what to expect from companies and when to expect it. The same principle of consistency also applies to other communications efforts, such as brochures, direct mail, and press relations.

In spite of the importance of consistency, it's probably the toughest brand-building requirement to implement. One reason is that *change* is endemic to this business, and change is the enemy of consistency. Market conditions change regularly. Products change rapidly. Competitors change the playing field with little or no warning. Companies are constantly reorganizing. While many of these changes are out of your control, all impact your ability to maintain some level of consistency around brand-building efforts.

What, then, can be done to better manage those activities over which you do have some control? Two things: first, think and act as if brand building were a cross-functional management task – more than just the responsibility of the marcom or marketing department; second, strive to develop a more systemic view of brand management.

Brand System Management

Brand proliferation is on the rise in most industries, including technology. As markets continue to fragment, more new products are introduced, and more line extensions are launched (or new brands are acquired), companies suddenly realize they have a confusing, overlapping, and nearly overwhelming number of brands to manage. In his book *Building Strong Brands*, Aaker does an excellent job of explaining how brands are functionally linked within an organization and how individual brand or product managers need to think and operate within the framework of a *brand system*.

Brands do not exist in isolation.

—DAVID AAKER,
BUILDING STRONG BRANDS

"A key to managing brands in an environment of complexity is to consider them not only as individual performers but also as members of a system of brands that must work to support one another. A brand system can serve as a launching platform for new products or brands and as a foundation for all brands in the system. But in order for the system to thrive, it must have a reciprocal relationship with each of its brands; they must support the system as much as the system supports them. Thinking in terms of a brand system also assists with resource allocation because it makes clear that a brand creates value by helping other brands in addition to generating its own value proposition. Thus a systems perspective adds the question of whether or not the whole system will benefit from a brand investment."[1]

It is important, however, not to think about the need for a brand system in an internal context only. Brands don't exist in isolation in the minds of customers either. Corporate brands, like HP, don't just stand alone; they also become an integral part of the LaserJet brand. In forming views and opinions about LaserJet, customers are affected by their perceptions of HP as well. And vice versa. It can get even more complex than that because LaserJet is also linked to DeskJet, and DeskJet is linked to DesignJet (and other related printer or imaging products), etc. Plus, dominant, successful subbrands like HP DeskJet can influence other HP subbrands aimed at similar target customers, like the HP Pavilion or HP Vectra personal computers.

Companies, therefore, need to view brand management not on an individual or *isolated* basis, but rather on a *systemic* basis. They need to understand the interrelationships between all brands and the dependencies of corporate brands on product, or subbrands, and vice versa. As they launch new products, companies need to understand that they are impacting not only the product brand but also the corporate brand and related subbrands. Properly managed, each successful product launch reinforces the brand it represents and strengthens the brand system. But approached in isolation, even successful product launches can do little to help build either the product or the corporate brand. Unsuccessful launches can negatively impact both. That's why it's important to ensure that product managers and other marketing personnel have proper exposure to – and training in – effective brand-building practices.

Hierarchy of Brand Meaning

One way to deal with this level of brand interrelationship and complexity is to apply a framework to help everyone involved in brand management better understand – from an outside or customer view – what role each brand or brand component plays in the overall brand system.

A key objective of branding is to attach some meaning to a product or series of products. This meaning is what is intended to be – and actually *is* – understood or experienced by a buyer of a particular product or service. In some cases, the meaning of a brand is little more than the actual product name, such as a component listing buried deep within a large catalog of basic electronic components. In others, the meaning of a brand is complex and rich with emotion, imagery, and experience. In practice, technology companies should strive to build meaning into their brands that:

- Provides information to customers
- Sets them apart from competitors
- Separates or complements brands within a company
- Conveys tangible and intangible reasons to buy

Meaning, like brand equity, lives at different *levels* for technology brands – from the corporate level to the current product level. Because of the complexity of technology products, the greater importance of some components over others, and the important role of company associations, managers face a real challenge in determining where to place proper emphasis when marketing products and crafting messages.

Figure 6-1

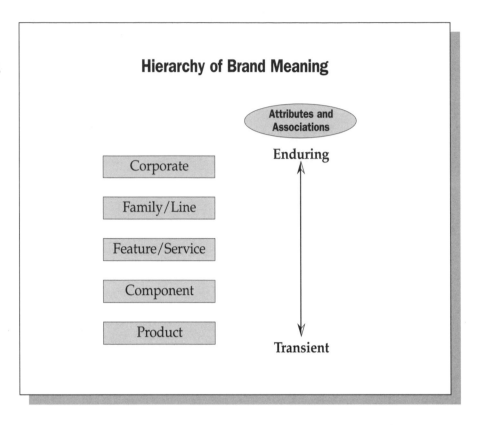

One guiding method is for marketers to first determine where that important and differentiating meaning "lives," whether at the corporate, product line, or individual product level. As Figure 6-1 illustrates, companies can utilize *hierarchy of brand meaning* as an approach to clarify where current brand meaning resides and what attributes and associations they want attached to their brands. This systems-oriented approach can help guide efforts to manage brands more effectively and efficiently.

Attributes and associations at the *corporate* level are powerful and enduring because they represent core company values. Microsoft, IBM, Apple, Sony, Novell, and Oracle have developed a number of basic and fundamental associations in the hearts and minds of customers over time. Some of these associations can be very beneficial, as "innovation" is to Sony or "ease of use" is to Apple; others can be limiting, as "arrogant" may be to Microsoft and "closed" may be to IBM. But these corporate-level associations collectively form the *meaning* and the equity customers come to attach to a brand at this level.

Meaning at the *family* or *line* or subbrand level starts to become more specific to a particular category of products. For Dell, each of the Dimension, OptiPlex, Latitude, and PowerEdge product lines plays

Figure 6-2

Dell Latitude Hierarchy of Meaning

	Brand/Model	Attributes and Associations
Corporate	Dell	Direct leader, responsive, different, customer-focused
Family/Line	Latitude	Dependable, high performance
Feature/Service	N/A	Focus on battery technology
Component	Intel Pentium	Widely recognized, quality CPU technology
Product	LMP133ST	Multimedia capability, affordable

specific subbrand roles within the overall brand system. Specific attributes and associations need to be conveyed to the marketplace for each — not only to differentiate from other product lines or product class competition but also to separate similar products within a given family. For example, the hierarchy of meaning for Dell's Latitude notebook line (see Figure 6-2) illustrates Dell's overall emphasis on the enduring values of "dependability" and "high performance" for the Latitude line, which allows an individual model, like the LM P133ST, to focus on specific product associations, in this case, multimedia capability. The collective meaning, of course, must be important to notebook customers and offer them some compelling reasons to buy Latitude instead of, for example, IBM's Thinkpad or Compaq's Armada (we'll further discuss brand-management challenges at this level in the section on subbrand management).

Meaning at the *features* and *service* level is another dimension for many technology products. IBM has attempted to brand its service capabilities and promote HelpLine as an added value to the desktop line. A few years ago, 3Com decided to brand a feature called Parallel Tasking. Up to that point, Parallel Tasking had been treated as a supporting feature for network products. Because it was a proprietary technology, 3Com felt that it should be elevated to a brand level of its own. So the company set out to develop a program to brand Parallel Tasking by creating recognition and meaning for the technology. It created an identity for Parallel Tasking, ran advertising to gain visibility, and created a co-op program to get partners to support brand-building efforts. Another example is the effort NEC has put behind CromaClear, the patented new monitor technology. If successful, this will add another level of meaning to the company's MultiSync line of monitors.

Component level is, of course, where Intel has succeeded so well. The "Intel Inside" program has added, for better or worse, another level of meaning to every PC participating in the program. Compaq actually stopped participating in the Intel program for a period of time because the company felt the meaning attached to the Intel processor was overshadowing the meaning it was building around the Compaq brand. On the other hand, Quantex, a lesser known direct-mail PC company, has positioned its brand by emphasizing "the finest, name-brand-only" components. While Intel is prominently featured, so are other recognized brands of CD-ROM drives, monitors, sound cards, modems, and graphics accelerators.

Component, or ingredient brand meaning, is also being utilized by many software companies, such as Cisco. According to Keith Fox, Vice President of Corporate Marketing, "Cisco IOS technology is a platform to enable network services. This is our ingredient software brand that allows us to tie together messages by market segments and accrue value back to our master Cisco brand." Unlike a *product* level of brand meaning, which can diminish or disappear as a product is discontinued, this software *component* level of brand meaning is meant to be quite enduring.

How To Use Brand Meaning

Every company should be able to create its own hierarchy of brand meaning for any brand in the system at any time. This exercise is beneficial to brand managers in many ways:

- **To aid in simplifying the brand message.** Generally, technology companies overcomplicate branding and offer too many choices and levels of meaning to customers. Customers are limited in their capacity to absorb too much meaning. When presented with such complexity, they screen out the superfluous and make selective judgments on what's important and familiar to them.

- **To help decide whether or not to introduce a new brand with the intention of building significant meaning around it.** The natural tendency for most product or brand managers is to come up with new brand names for new products. Often, this exercise will help them decide if that's a smart decision or not. One major printer company recently performed this type of assessment for its inkjet line and decided not to create a prominent new subbrand to support a launch into new markets. The consensus was that the current line name, together with a new model designation, would be simpler and a more cost-effective way to leverage existing brand equity.

- **To guide planning and positioning strategy around the current set of brands.** For example, making sure products are properly "distanced" from each other within family groups. A company like Toshiba could benefit from this exercise by examining its extensive number of portable subbrands. The results could determine if there's too much meaning for customers to reasonably absorb and if the subbrands collectively are more confusing than clarifying.

- **To guide in the development of naming conventions.** After reviewing the hierarchy of meaning for its product line-up, the HP Colorado Memory Systems division decided to keep a simple numeric model-naming convention for future new products, rather than introduce new names. This route was chosen in order not to detract from existing efforts to build primary recognition and brand meaning at the higher HP Colorado *corporate* and *family/line* levels.

- **To guide investment decisions for new brand launches.** If new products can "borrow" from meaning that already exists at the corporate or family level, it becomes easier for managers to determine how much effort is necessary to create any newly desired meaning. When HP made a more aggressive move into the storage market with the SureStore line, the company decided it didn't need to emphasize trust and stability at the *line* level, as those attributes and meaning already existed at the HP *corporate* level. Thus, managers decided to focus on creating more specific meaning around SureStore benefits associated with specific storage line-level attributes like expertise, innovation, and ease of use.

Subbrand Management

Subbrands, by definition, are virtually the same as line or family brands in that they "live" under the corporate brand umbrella. Interestingly, subbrand management has resulted in more ongoing controversy and consternation inside technology companies during the past several years than perhaps any other aspect of brand management. When the business-oriented personal computer market first began to expand into consumer markets in the late 1980's, several manufacturers started to broaden existing product lines, creating distinct subbrands in order to address the unique needs of these markets and to minimize concern over channel conflict resulting from selling similar or exact products at different prices through different channels.

Over time, however, as companies continued to expand even further into distinct market segments, or subsegments, such as the home *office* segment or the *mobile* office segment, subbrands began to proliferate industrywide. Sub-subbrands even appeared, such as the Compaq Contura Aero. Many companies pushed brand-naming conventions to the edge, and, for some, it was actually over the edge. Near the peak of the PC subbranding frenzy a few years ago, *The Wall Street Journal* featured an article entitled "Too Many Computer Names Confuse Too Many Buyers." Included was an inset section inviting readers to "Test your PC knowledge and match the top PC manufacturers with their models." Naturally, most people who took the challenge could not correctly associate all the subbrands with their actual parent brands.

At this same time, many PC companies began to realize that having too many subbrands was possibly not the best way to leverage opportunities in the market. G. Richard Thoman of IBM proclaimed, "We've introduced needless complexity." Shortly thereafter, IBM announced a new branding strategy that reduced the number of PC subbrands from nine to four. One of the brands eliminated was Ambra, which had been created specifically to reach a distinct consumer-market segment that presumably was not predisposed to buying IBM products. According to Abby Kohnstamm, IBM's Vice President of Corporate Marketing, "Ambra was a terrible failure. It would have been better to reach out with an existing IBM brand to this customer set versus going after them with yet another clone brand."

Other companies have taken longer to arrive at a similar subbranding conclusion. In the summer of 1996, Compaq announced a significant reduction in subbrands, including the consolidation of all portable computer products under a single subbrand, the Compaq Armada. Jim Garrity of Compaq explains how the company arrived at its decision: "We became convinced over time that we had too many subbrands, that we weren't making it easy for customers to make choices and to understand what each product line stood for, that we weren't getting good name recognition uniformly at the subbrand level. Because we had so many, we couldn't afford to invest sufficiently in all of them... so we concluded that we had too many mouths to feed and we'd be much better served by having fewer subbrands."

While Compaq's decision to reduce the number of subbrands is quite logical and correctly views the decision from a *customer* perspective, other companies have yet to acknowledge or are slow to recognize that consumers cannot make so many distinctions between competitive products, let alone between a single vendor's different subbrands. Fujitsu, a latecomer to the portable computer market, launched its first line of notebooks under the Fujitsu brand with three separate subbrands, the Milano, the Monte Carlo, and the Montego. Although some people may have been impressed with the cleverness of these names, and Fujitsu spent several million dollars in advertising all three subbrands, the company ultimately concluded that it was unwise to try to establish three separate notebook subbrands and consolidated all portables under a single subbrand, the Fujitsu Lifebook.

Managing Corporate Identity

As we discussed in the brand-building and management guidelines section, *consistency* builds strong brands. Consistency in messages *and* consistency in look across the entire spectrum of communications vehicles are what help build strong brands and build them more rapidly. One key method to promote and ensure brand image consistency is through the development and implementation of a corporate-identity program.

Corporate-identity programs vary in scope and complexity – from simple to complex. Some are merely graphic standards manuals that illustrate how to size and apply the corporate signature and/or logo. Others are exhaustive corporate-identity systems that fully define proper and improper usage and offer guidelines for every conceivable identity manifestation. The more comprehensive programs provide direction and guidance for proper application of corporate identity in a broad array of identity usages, including business papers such as business cards, business forms (electronic or printed), labels, and letterhead; product names and designations; documentation; marketing communications materials such as advertising and collateral; specialty or "premium" items; news releases; packaging and documentation; presentations; and signage and displays (e.g. on buildings or at trade shows).

By defining the proper application of corporate identity, these guidelines facilitate the development of a consistent, uniform image for the brand that builds brand recognition and enhances the brand's identity. Inconsistent usage, on the other hand, leads to customer confusion and can undermine other branding efforts and the overall development of the brand. Sometimes, even when companies have extensive published guidelines, it becomes difficult to ensure proper usage, especially on a global basis. One of the ways that companies are addressing this challenge is by leveraging available technology to disseminate appropriate identity standards and guidelines electronically, whether on floppy disks, CD-ROM, or, most dynamically, via the company Intranet. This latter method is probably the most advantageous, since it permits regional entities to more easily follow and update the appropriate standards in their respective languages.

Global Brand Management

No chapter on brand management would be complete without a discussion of global or multi-national branding. In fact, it could be the subject of an entire book, because the topic is so complex and controversial. Both of us have worked in large, multi-national technology companies and had global brand responsibilities. We're very familiar with the various challenges and pitfalls associated with global brand management – like the trade-offs between centralized corporate control and regional autonomy, developing global campaigns utilizing common creative versus a country-by-country development process, and maintaining consistent brand-identity elements – in addition to managing the ongoing struggles to gain consensus on priorities and equitable budget allocations.

While no absolutes exist, a few time-tested key principles should be kept in mind:

- Don't mistake global branding for inflexible dictates or uniform solutions that must be applied without variation in different markets.
- While powerful brands thrive with consistency, consistency in this case does not mean uniformity.
- At the same time, branding also needs to be flexible and responsive to local needs and requirements. Managers have to take into account not only cultural differences but also local market conditions, legal restrictions, competitive challenges, buying habits, and distribution realities.

As Figure 6-3 shows, successful branding on a global basis is all about striking a balance between global consistency and integrity and local relevance and flexibility.

You should strive for the elements of consistency that are core to the brand: enduring values, mission, positioning (on a value-proposition level), and identity. Some of the strongest technology brands around the world today – Compaq, Microsoft, Apple, and IBM – achieve brand strength, in part, because they get enormous leverage on a country-to-country basis from a single, consistent core identity and enduring brand values. Smart global brand management also recognizes that, to a large degree, local hands should guide tactical execution of local messages, allocation of the communications mix, and target audience selection, as well as exercise control over their respective budgets. This is a delicate balancing act that must be worked out with regional representatives in a spirit of cooperation for the good of the brand.

While IBM consolidated all of its advertising under a single agency, which enables it to achieve very consistent campaigns on a worldwide

Figure 6-3

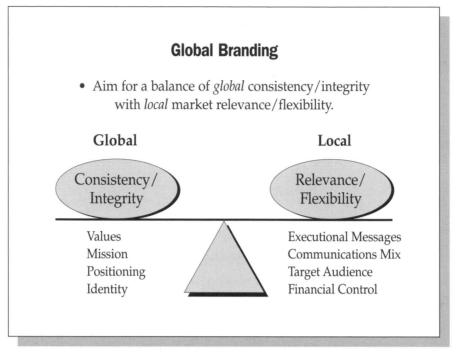

Global Branding

- Aim for a balance of *global* consistency/integrity with *local* market relevance/flexibility.

Global	Local
Consistency/Integrity	Relevance/Flexibility
Values	Executional Messages
Mission	Communications Mix
Positioning	Target Audience
Identity	Financial Control

basis, most companies do not have the size, presence, or resources required to pull off such a centralized brand-management approach, even if they wanted to try. Though Compaq is large enough to centralize brand management, it has opted for a more decentralized approach to global brand management. The various regions and their representative agencies meet on a quarterly basis to work toward the ongoing development of a strong Compaq brand. As Jim Garrity puts it: "What we've been able to accomplish has been through a collaborative set of processes and regular forums with the heads of marcom from each of our five regions. We have formed a 'virtual' global corporate marcom organization in the absence of a formal one and this has served us very well."

In this whole discussion, the key to remember is that brand success and brand equity live in the hearts and minds of individual customers. For that reason, local representatives can generally play a more important role in how those individual customers, on a country-by-country basis, come to perceive a brand.

In this chapter, we examined brand management and brand building from a detailed systems and structural perspective. In the next chapter, we will explore a variety of *PowerBranding* strategies.

7

PowerBranding™ Strategies

I believe the successor to brand image in the Post Present will be the Brand Experience, which goes beyond the attributes of the product.

– LESTER WUNDERMAN,
Being Direct: How I Learned To Make Advertising Pay

Positioning is making the best of what a brand is, not trying to make it into something else.

– TIM AMBLER,
Marketing from Advertising to Zen

Theodore Levitt was the first to express the idea that the real purpose of business was not to make a profit but to acquire and keep customers. Technology companies have generally tended to focus more attention and resources on customer acquisition than on customer retention. How many times during marketing planning meetings has the thought "we need to retain more of our current customers" come up as a goal? Not very often, because, for many companies, the emphasis is generally on getting new customers. This orientation toward "customer conquest" plays out in different ways.

For hardware companies, the quest for new customers has been largely driven by rapid product obsolescence that impels customers to constantly upgrade their systems and, at each upgrade cycle, to potentially consider a new vendor. Software companies, while doing a better job of focusing on customer retention, especially when soliciting customers to upgrade to new releases, have also typically placed more attention on gaining new customers and expanding the customer base.

In recent years, on-line brands like America Online (AOL) have focused on getting as many new customers as possible. Until recently, AOL's primary marketing efforts seemed to be a massive blanketing of every conceivable person in the country with free trial offers (e.g. a Reno Air version of the promotion bundles an AOL floppy disk with the in-flight snack). While part of this was due to the churn rates experienced by on-line service providers, this main focus was necessary to get to a "critical mass" of customers in order to support the changing and challenging business model. Lacking a sufficient base of customers, Prodigy exited the traditional on-line service business, only to be reincarnated as an Internet service. Other software companies like McAfee have had success with a more risky, but ultimately effective, customer-acquisition strategy – to first give the product away, then charge a subscription fee to customers who stay with certain company products.

Brand Strategy: Getting, Keeping, and Growing Customers

To some extent, this predominant conquest approach worked fine when the computer market was growing rapidly and new customers were relatively easy to find. But this mind-set of viewing marketing's job as constantly bringing new customers into the fold has often led to the neglect of current customers. Some companies have primarily viewed customer retention not as a marketing function but as a customer service function. Recently, the balance has shifted somewhat, and the significance of retention is now recognized for what it really is – an important part of the marketing job. And, as David Arnold argues, since marketing and branding are virtually synonymous, customer retention becomes a brand strategist's job, too. That's why, as we mentioned earlier, brand loyalty is now getting a lot more attention in technology companies. It's also why, as Figure 7-1 illustrates, brand strategy must incorporate brand-relationship activities that focus as much on keeping – and growing – customers, as on acquiring them. New marketing thinking now recognizes that share of *customer* may be more important than share of *market*. Microsoft already thinks about growth opportunities in terms of how to obtain more revenue per personal computer customer. So, brand strategists have to extend their thinking horizontally, along the entire brand experience continuum.

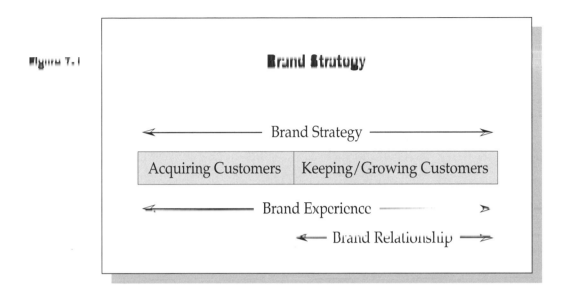

Figure 7-1

In addressing *PowerBranding* strategies, we want to be clear that we are taking a broad and holistic view. Brand strategy is not just about how many customers we can bring into the fold. Smart brand strategy is really about how many *profitable* customers we can attract and how we can retain them longer or even grow them. Any discussion about brand strategy, then, must be in the context of the fundamental business purpose of acquiring, retaining, and growing customers. As Figure 7-1 indicates, a well-developed and managed brand experience is one of the first strategies to help achieve this goal.

Brand Experience

To date, no technology company has done a better job of marketing the brand experience than Apple. Right from the early days, Apple intuitively recognized the importance of creating a rich, emotional context for and around its products. Its communications adroitly combined promises of nebulous, yet appealing, ideas like "empowerment" (i.e. "the power to be your best") with substantial product information. Apple conveyed a differentiating and consistent attitude, look, and feel, as well as a tight focus on key messages throughout its marketing efforts of the 1980's. The company also practically invented the idea of turning technology product introductions into major public events, a practice commonly referred to as "event marketing."

Even today, as Apple struggles to regain its footing in the vastly changed computer marketplace, presumably dispassionate business writers still use language like "the Apple mystique" when reporting on the company. It's a testimony to the strength and the enduring benefits of a special brand experience, which helps Apple retain strong brand equity, in spite of product problems and fundamental marketplace shifts. As David Roman, Apple's Vice President for Corporate Advertising and Brand Marketing, puts it: "The one thing that made us different and still makes us different is the relationship that users have with our products. We call it the "smile factor" (in reference to the icon that greets users upon power-up). The user *experience* has been what's driven this feeling about the Apple brand."

The concept of brand experience is based on a simple premise: a brand is not really known by a customer from the mere reception of messages, but rather from the collective *encounters* – large and small – with the brand over time. These encounters shape perceptions and opinions of brands. And, as Tom Peters has said, "Perception is all there is. What customers perceive in their experiences with products and services and their contacts with employees is real; it must be listened to, understood and acted upon."[2]

Les Wunderman, cited at the beginning of this chapter, has a keen appreciation for the importance of the total brand experience. He defines the brand experience as "a gestalt that includes the packaging, the advertising, where and how the product is sold, the price, the consumer's satisfaction from its use, the service provided, the continuous renewal of the product's uniqueness, and the development of an interactive relationship that bonds the buyer and seller after the sale is made."[3]

When you think of a brand in the larger framework of promising and delivering a special *experience*, as opposed to a more limiting, purely functional view or a traditional image view of a brand, it takes on more

Marketing in a post-industrial society is not a marketing of function, it is a marketing of experience.[1]

– JOHN SCULLY,
FORMER APPLE CEO

92

importance. Microsoft, according to Greg Perlot, is "certainly branding at the experience level because software has some real advantages there, and that's what we're striving for – a Microsoft experience." And it applies to hardware, too.

Consider the Dell brand. For a long time, many people (not Dell customers) underestimated what the Dell brand experience was all about. Skeptics believed it had mostly to do with direct distribution of good clone PCs at lower prices. They only saw the obvious part. The Dell brand, however, has always stood for the promise of a better customer *experience* of buying and owning a PC. That experience includes easy and convenient purchase of a quality, custom-built computer that offers the latest technology at a reasonable (but not necessarily the lowest) price – and which is backed by excellent service and support. Not just a promise of excellent service, but the actual *delivery* of and experience of superior support, time and time again (as consistently verified by a number of independent customer-satisfaction surveys). Dell was, and is, able to promise a better customer experience because of its direct customer relationship that forms the foundation of the Dell brand experience. Also, the company has continuously refined its systems and capabilities, while also training personnel to deliver a better experience.

We're not certain why – maybe it's the nature of their service business, but airline companies seem to understand the concept of brand experience very well. Jan Carlzon, former CEO of SAS, expresses his view of the brand experience in his book *Moments of Truth*. His belief is that perceptions of the SAS brand are shaped by nearly 50 million customer contacts a year, each lasting, on average, just 15 seconds. He also believes that these little "moments of truth" not only shape the SAS brand experience but also determine the ultimate success or failure of the company.

When interviewed, Sir Colin Marshall, Chairman of British Airways, had this to say about the company's brand experience:

"There are different ways to think about how to compete. One way is to think that a business is merely performing a function – in our case, transporting people from point a to point b and at the lowest possible price. That's the commodity mind-set. Another way to compete is to go beyond the function and compete on the basis of providing an experience. In our case, we want to make the process of flying from a to b as effortless and pleasant as possible.

We strive to make our customers' travel experience seamless, personal and caring. We see the product not simply as a seat but more comprehensively as an experience being orchestrated across the airline. That orchestration is the brand."[4]

The contrast between a service-oriented business like the airline industry and a more tangible, product-based business like the technology industry is obvious. But the difference is more of degree than kind. Brand experience in this industry is not limited to whether or not the product performs well. Brand experience is all about the totality of what's promised and what's delivered throughout the customer's or user's engagement with the brand. Powerful technology brands achieve the *power brand* status because they have come to represent a special, desirable, and positive experience for the customer. That experience is not just around the actual performance of the product; it's about how the customer feels about the company behind the product; how hassle-free the product was to buy, install, or set up; and how quickly any problems were resolved.

Brand strategists, then, should pay close attention to what we call creating or promising the *differentiating brand experience*. The more you can create some brand recognition in the area of differentiated, personal, and emotional experiences, the better your chance to win. The greatest opportunities for enduring brand success happen when you are able to orchestrate the range of experiences around your brand in a way that puts your brand in a more personal and emotional space. This happens only when the promise of a brand rises above the merely functional and tangible and incorporates some relevant feeling and emotion. Competitors can match functions and features, but they can't easily match the promise and delivery of a personal, emotional, and special experience.

Iomega, primarily through its brand-building efforts for the Zip and Ditto removable storage devices, has managed to place its brands in a very different space from other storage products. This was accomplished in innovative ways that moved the products into the differentiated space of personal and emotional experiences, rather than remain in the rational, impersonal, and undifferentiated area that removable drive makers (including Iomega) had traditionally occupied (for a detailed examination of this brand reinvention, see Chapter 9). That's an important lesson for brand strategists in understanding the concept of a differentiating brand experience.

Design As a Key Part of the Differentiating Brand Experience

Recently, technology companies have more enthusiastically embraced design as an important and differentiating component of the overall brand experience. Of course, some companies, most notably Apple, have known this for years. Apple has had a strong design sensibility right from the start. Its innovative designs for Macintosh and later products went beyond interesting form factors and helped define the Apple brand identity in important ways. Similarly, Logitech has instilled a strong design ethic into its mouse and other input and control devices that sets the company apart from competitors. In part, this is due to Co-founder Pierluigi Zappacosta's intuitive understanding of the importance of creative design in business. Because of Logitech's unique designs, customers have come to appreciate and value the subtle, but satisfying, way the products blend form and function.

In an increasingly undifferentiated PC market, many companies like Acer, Compaq, IBM, and Packard Bell have also used product design to set their products apart from the crowd. When Packard Bell felt it needed an image boost, the company first considered a multi-million dollar advertising campaign on T.V. Instead, it decided to hire Frog Design, a leading industrial design firm, to overhaul the product line. For a while, the new, differentiated designs worked to help the company stand out and improve its image. But, ultimately, they were not enough to compensate for other competitive weaknesses (such as a reputation for inferior service and unreliability) that resulted in a less-than-satisfactory overall customer experience. Acer, in positioning products for the home market, has emphasized design and color as important parts of its appeal to new customers. Initial advertising for the Aspire 2000 series, for example, conveyed a feeling of a fashionably designed product with the line "Available in charcoal and emerald. Sorry, no beige."

With these and other success stories as evidence that design can lead to true differentiation, more technology companies (even software companies in terms of design elements present in the user interface and functional icons) should consider improving and leveraging innovative aspects of design as part of their overall brand strategy.

Extending the Brand Experience

As we discussed in Chapter 1's section on Brand Power, it's difficult to become a well-known brand if a customer cannot see or experience your product (i.e. it's merely a component such as a power supply, hidden inside a larger product like a PC). Of course, as Intel has demonstrated, even components can promise a brand experience with the sheer weight of investment in impactful, broad-based communications. Intel has been able to give its microprocessor a distinct personality, establishing "the computer inside" as the animated brain of a computer (the ongoing series of animated commercials certainly helps in this regard).

However, it's not necessary, or even practical, for many companies to spend millions of dollars to achieve some level of brand recognition. The *brand experience*, properly understood, can lead to novel strategies that help a company overcome inherent product limitations. Iomega, as we mentioned, redefined the entire category of portable storage with its Zip drive. Previous to the product's introduction, most computer users didn't think much about the "identity" of their storage devices. By positioning the Zip drive in a benefit-oriented, consumer fashion – the place to "store all your stuff"– Iomega created a strong association for the Zip device as a truly personal tool. This facilitated a deeper connection with the customer and a deeper brand experience, which, in turn, led to the rapid formation of a unique brand identity and a rapid increase in sales.

Another example of extending the brand experience in a novel way is what Canon Computer Systems did with the Bubble Jet line of inkjet printers. Historically, printers were viewed as inanimate peripheral products – a combination of hardware, silicon, and ink that printed documents created by software. But viewing the printer from a customer point of view, Canon saw how it could enhance both the product offering and the customer experience with the product. Canon then began to include software and offer add-on products that enabled customers to create and print greeting cards, custom brochures, personalized t-shirts, etc. This resulted in a higher level of personal interaction and a deeper customer relationship with the brand. As Norman Hajjar, President and CEO of Hajjar and Partners, Canon's advertising agency, puts it: "Because of the level of interaction with the products, based upon their daily use and upon what users can accomplish and actually do with Canon printers, the potential to affect the perception and strength of the brand is a lot greater than with other products, such as copiers. This type of customer interaction is more powerful because of its very personal nature."

Brand Positioning and Brand-Value Proposition

Positioning is an enduring, time-tested concept that existed in marketing strategy lexicon well before it was popularized in the 1980's by Trout and Ries in their now-classic book, *Positioning: The Battle For Your Mind*. Even though positioning is a well-researched concept, technology brand builders are still cautioned to apply the concept judiciously. Why?

For one reason, the positioning concept originated at a time when markets moved a lot slower, when competitors stood still long enough for a marketer to get a bead on them, when media was less fractionated, and when consumers were more homogeneous. While basic positioning concepts obviously still have merit, the unique dynamics of the technology marketplace require a different approach to the positioning challenge.

Brand positioning is about claiming a distinct space in the marketplace, i.e. one that is differentiated from the competition *and* meaningful to the customer. But determining a good brand positioning alone is not a sufficient brand strategy. What's more effective is first defining the fundamental *brand-value proposition* – then defining the brand position as an expression of your brand value proposition. Together, the brand-value proposition and the brand positioning comprise a more complete brand strategy.

A brand-value proposition is not simply a positioning statement dressed up a bit. It's the strategic statement that sums up the specific *quality* and *nature* of the relationship between the brand and the customer. It's the statement that sets a brand apart from its competitors and drives purchase decisions. As David Aaker defines it: "A brand's value proposition is a statement of the functional, emotional and self-expressive benefits delivered by the brand that provide value to the customer."[6]

In this definition, Aaker makes some useful distinctions about the different types of benefits brands can, and should, provide. Functional benefits are those directly linked to some product attribute, such as speed, power, capability, or performance. Emotional benefits are those that result in positive feelings by a customer. They can often be linked to functional benefits, and, in fact, Aaker asserts that the strongest brands provide both functional and emotional benefits. For example, HP LaserJet printers stand for quality and reliability, but they also provide emotional reassurances that you can count on them not to let you down in the middle of an important job. Self-expressive benefits are subtly different from emotional benefits in that they are more about what a brand purchase says about the buyer. Case in point, Apple buyers, at least early on, felt that buying Apple and Macintosh computers was, in part, an expression of their individuality. Today's powerful notebook computers, ranging in cost up to $10,000 or more, can also have self-expressive benefits ("notebook envy" is a term used to describe the feeling one gets when discovering that another airline passenger possesses an even newer and more powerful model).

What Is a Good Brand-Value Proposition?

A brand-value proposition is not typically a tight, three-word expression. It's also important not to confuse a tagline with a brand-value proposition. "Solutions for a small planet" and "Where do you want to go today?" are IBM's and Microsoft's taglines – they're creative expressions of more fundamental values and promises of benefits. Good value propositions, on the other hand, provide proper, long-term direction for what you want to stand for as a brand. In the case of Microsoft, the tagline is an expression of the fundamental brand-value proposition of "access," with the promise that "Microsoft leads the way in providing access to the new world of thinking and communicating."

Also, just because the term "brand-value proposition" includes the word "value," don't think there should be a price reference in the proposition. An appealing price can be, and often is, part of the brand-value statement for companies wanting to gain recognition and compete, at least partially, on a price basis. Generally, good brand-value statements focus on other, more differentiating benefits. Anyway, products are not considered for purchase without also taking price into account. Good brand-value propositions create the context for your price to play the proper (i.e. not dominating) role when customers are actually considering the product for purchase.

To help determine what is a good brand-value proposition, we have developed this simple 10-point test:

- **Consistent.** Is the proposition consistent with, and supportive of, the overall corporate brand strategy, including the company's mission and vision?
- **Motivating.** Is the promise of the proposition relevant and motivating to the target audience?
- **Differentiating.** Does the promise set your brand apart from the competition on some meaningful basis?
- **Deliverable.** Is the benefit (or benefits) something you can actually deliver to the customer?
- **Sustainable.** Can you continue to deliver this benefit and will it continue to be differentiating over time?
- **Targeted.** Is it focused on a well-defined target audience?
- **Honest.** Is the proposition honest, believable, and consistent with the character of the company?
- **Simple.** Is the statement simple to express, easy to explain, and hard to misinterpret?
- **Supported.** Is the proposition understood and supported internally with enthusiasm and commitment?
- **Leveragable.** Can the proposition be applied to a range of products and services that supports a growing, dynamic brand – or is it limited to specific product offerings?

Brand Identity or Brand Image?

This is another area where semantics often gets in the way of understanding the true nature of brand building. Brand identity is often used in a limited, graphic-centric manner or used interchangeably with brand image. All too often, identity is seen as just the graphics, logos, colors, and symbols that generally make up corporate identity. Those elements are the appearance (which is very important) but not the substance of a brand, just as the clothes you wear are an important, even distinguishing, part of your identity but not the substance of who you are as a person. Interesting discussions in business books and marketing circles debate this very thing – image versus identity. For our purposes, it's useful to summarize the discussion and present our point of view. Again, language makes a difference. If top executives hear the words "brand identity" or "brand image" and immediately think of something quite different than is intended, it's often hard to make any progress in advancing the brand-building cause.

Here's a simple way to sum up and understand the two terms: image is how the marketplace perceives you; identity is who you really are. According to Jean-Noel Kapferer, "Identity precedes image. An obsession with image tends to attach greater importance to appearance than to inner reality. But brand identity is a richer, more substantial concept to embrace."[7] David Aaker agrees: "Brand identity is a unique set of brand associations that the brand strategist aspires to create or maintain. These associations represent what the brand stands for and imply a promise from the organization's members."[8]

As shown in Figure 7-2, we can even further clarify and contrast the important differences between brand image and brand identity:

Figure 7-2

Brand Image Versus Brand Identity

Brand Image	Brand Identity
Appearance	Substance
More on the receiver's side	More on the sender's side
Passive	Active
Reflects superficial qualities	Reflects enduring qualities
Backward looking	Forward looking
Tactical	Strategic
Associations already here	Associations aspired to

We recommend that companies focus on building brand identity as the driving brand-strategy component. Brand image is not to be diminished at all. It is, after all is said and done, how the market perceives you. But don't make the mistake of thinking your brand image is your identity. The challenge for brand strategists and champions is to align image and identity. That happens – and can only happen – by careful, proactive management of your brand-identity components. First know what your image is in the marketplace today and how it is not aligned with what your brand really is or with the identity you desire. Then do what you can to try to fix it with the resources available.

Components of Brand Identity

If brand identity is how a brand really is or wants to be perceived, then what are the key components of brand identity? They are names, symbols, brand personality, associations, and attributes. These components provide the cues and messages customers use to define and understand what a brand is really all about.

Names and Symbols

When the lights go down and the microphone goes on, it doesn't matter what your name is.

—THE ARTIST FORMERLY KNOWN AS PRINCE

When it comes to names, not all technology brands are in the same position as the popular artist now known by the symbol of an unpronounceable glyph. And they wouldn't necessarily want to be. Names are obviously important because they do make a long-term difference. If you had the choice, would you spend $10 billion for the Coke name (and formula, of course) or $5 billion for the company's plant and distribution system? It isn't so much the name itself but what that name represents and means to customers. The artist just mentioned has simply taken that idea to an extreme. He wants to be known – as a symbol only – for his substance, not his name. Indeed, a few companies – Nike, Mercedes, and even Apple – have also reached a point where they can merely show a symbol and customers automatically know and appreciate the brand meaning and substance behind that symbol. That's a powerful position, but most technology companies don't achieve that stature with their names.

Names are both cues for brand associations and magnets for brand meaning. They have to be chosen carefully and constantly monitored as they age. The name "Compaq," initially selected because it combined word elements of computer and compact, was appropriate for a smaller, portable alternative to IBM. Over time, Compaq successfully diminished the early "size" association and replaced it with one of quality and reliability, which allowed the name to broadly extend its appeal. Sometimes it's not easy to get the name right from the start. PC's Limited became better known as Dell Computer when Founder Michael Dell made the fortuitous switch to a simpler, more obvious name. Oracle started out as Relational Systems, Inc. and later adopted the name of its best-selling product. Apple was an inspired brand-name choice from the beginning. Not only did it reflect the counter-IBM culture of a feisty start-up, but it also was immediately distinctive and memorable. Plus, it came ahead of then-rival Atari in an alphabetical listing – a small, but important, distinction at the time.

The key point is to treat name as one of the most important strategic elements of your brand-building efforts. Apply *PowerBranding* principles to the task – such as bringing a customer-centric view, not just a product-oriented one. Consider how the name can support the mission. Take a long-term view. All too often technology company executives – founders especially – believe they can save money by doing the naming themselves. Or they have an inspiration for a name that sounds great to them and/or their friends. Our advice is not to succumb to that temptation. Get expert advice right from the start. Names are the most visible and often most permanent part of the brand identity; they need to be selected objectively and in a systematic, disciplined manner.

Symbols, as logos or design elements or whatever, also play a key role in brand strategy. Symbols can communicate associations, generate some comforting familiarity and positive feelings, and enhance identity. The cocky way Dell tilts the "e" in its name toward the "d" reinforces an attitude of doing things just a little differently from the rest of the pack. Pictures of spotted cows, first used in a whimsical way in Gateway advertising, have become an inseparable part of the company's identity. As Jim Taylor, Gateway's Senior Vice President of Worldwide Marketing, said in an interview for *Fast Company* magazine, "It's hard to describe what an advantage those silly cow-spotted boxes are. People just love them." For Gateway, cows have become part of the friendly, unassuming, and folksy identity the company wants to express. But the cow-spotted boxes are more than just a symbol; they are also part of Gateway's brand personality.

Brand Personality

Brand personality is the aspect of identity that reflects the persona of the brand. Because it's intangible and exists in an emotional realm, personality is often underrated by technology marketers. That can be a significant oversight. A recognizable and well-defined brand personality is a key part of a successful brand's richness, distinctiveness, and appeal. Often, it's what breaks the tie in the purchase-decision process when all the rational merits of two competitive products are deemed equal.

Personality is often used interchangeably with terms like brand tone, manner, or character. Generally, it's expressed in personal or character terms – trustworthy, energetic, assertive, unpretentious, arrogant, friendly, helpful, and so on. As brands become more familiar to customers, they tend to take on these human qualities and characteristics, for better or worse. In addition, personality will come through even if you don't intend for it to. Since it can be the best place to create some lasting differentiation, it pays to develop a well thought-out brand personality description as part of the brand-identity strategy.

Brand-personality statements are often created to facilitate a part of advertising development. In such cases, the statement should reflect and support the overall brand personality. While advertising is frequently the most visible aspect, it's not the entirety of the brand's personality. Personality comes from many cues around the brand experience. Boring, tasteless, or cheap ads will help shape an unattractive brand personality. A cumbersome software user interface detracts from a positive brand personality. Packaging that constantly changes or lacks a quality appearance sets certain, but unhelpful, expectations about the character of the brand. On the flip side, packaging can, and should, help communicate and support positive personality aspects of the brand. Poor handling of customer service also affects brand personality to some degree. Ultimately, nearly every interaction with a customer shapes the brand personality.

Personalities can be very differentiating, especially at the corporate level. As we discussed earlier, corporate-level brand attributes are becoming more and more important in the purchase process for technology products. IDG's Wave VI research, *Brands and the Buying Process*, provided insight into how computer buyers rate various hardware and software companies on a variety of personality dimensions.

Figure 7-3

Rating of Corporate Brand Personality Profiles on Top Five Attributes*

HP	Trustworthy (25%), Cares about what customers think (21%), Smart/Savvy (17%), Technology leadership (16%), Successful (16%)
Intel	Visionary (28%), Technology leadership (26%), Successful (24%), Innovative (20%), Smart/Savvy (20%)
Apple	Cool/Hip (37%), Innovative (27%), Down to earth/Friendly (27%), Visionary (24%), Cares about what customers think (16%)
IBM	Not as good as they used to be (37%), Trustworthy (27%), Technology leadership (27%), Smart/Savvy (22%), Successful (20%)
Compaq	Trustworthy (12%), Cares about what customers think (10%), Smart/Savvy (10%), Successful (9%), Technology leadership (7%)
Microsoft	Successful (91%), Technology leadership (75%), Smart/Savvy (71%), Visionary (71%), Innovative (69%)
Novell	Down to earth/Friendly (23%), Cares about what customers think (23%), Trustworthy (20%), Not as good as they used to be (16%), Smart/Savvy (12%)

*Chart lists the percentage of respondents rating each company on the various attributes.

As shown in Figure 7-3, HP came across as confident, considerate, and human. Intel was seen as a visionary leader but lacking a softer side, with only a 2% rating on "Down to Earth/Friendly." Apple stood out, as expected, for its cool and hip attitude. IBM was perceived with a somewhat split personality, reflecting perceptions of both the difficult times of the early 1990's and the company's recent resurgence. Compaq was notable not by any one characteristic but by how low their overall personality profile registered. The traditional focus on product features gave the company strong associations with functional attributes but not much of a human side, something the company has been working on recently (e.g. "Has it changed your life yet?"). Microsoft, not surprisingly, dominated nearly all of the positive personality attributes for the software companies rated.

One thing that's important and perhaps unique to this industry is that certain aspects of corporate brand personality can come from the high-profile company founders. This presents interesting challenges for these companies. The most obvious example is Bill Gates, who's "a brand himself," according to Greg Perlot. In the customer's mind, Gates' strong image and presence also represents Microsoft. That was part of the reason Microsoft moved more aggressively to shape its corporate brand identity in 1994. Oracle is another example. As Zach Nelson, Senior Vice President for Marketing, says: "Oracle-ness" has been defined more by default than intent. And it's been embodied by Larry Ellison. It's aggressive, sales-focused and competitive driven. Now, there's more of a customer focus coming through." Again, Oracle is taking proactive steps to manage its identity, rather than accept the current image that exists in the hearts and minds of many customers and potential customers.

Here as some additional considerations for brand personality development:

- **Don't underestimate the importance of a likable personality.** Liking the brands and all that the brand represents is an underrated part of the technology purchase process. As brand-identity authority Lynn Upshaw says, "Likability is a key plank in the bridge that should be built between customer and brand. It's one of the most important lures any brand can offer."[9] IBM is trying very hard to present a more human side to its brand personality – in part, to be seen as friendlier and more likable and thus counteract the impersonal image that persists.

- **Don't underrate brand personality.** Personalities in brands, just like in people, attract certain types of people. Trying to appeal to everybody should be avoided. Some of the more distinctive brand personalities succeed because they don't try to be all things to all people. Gateway is a good example.

- **Don't be misled by research that appears to diminish the role of personality.** Most quantitative research will point out, and rightly so, that functional attributes are what really drive consideration and purchase. However, those left-brain attributes also happen to be the easiest to measure in a research setting. It's tough to get at the true importance of emotional, right-brain intangibles like personality in structured research. Yet, we know they make a difference. Qualitative research, however, can help companies better understand the personalities of brands and the roles they play.

Associations and Attributes

Brand associations and attributes are those specific aspects or dimensions that a potential buyer uses to make judgments about the benefits of, and differences between, brand alternatives. It's the job of the brand strategist to identify motivating and differentiating associations (within the context of the brand-value proposition and identity goals) and strive, through brand management and brand-building efforts, to have customers attach those associations to the brand. Associations, of course, can be functional or intangible, and they have varying degrees of importance to different people.

Here are some important considerations:

- **Be aware of what some call "the attributes or features as benefits trap."** Attributes and features can lead to benefits. But attributes alone, such as "high performance," are not necessarily benefits. When they are expressed in customer-benefit terms and experienced by the customer as benefits, desirable associations can become attached to brands. Desktop PC products that aim for a "high reliability" *attribute*, for example, can communicate the *benefits* of higher work productivity or a lower cost of ownership.
- **Recognize that both corporate-level attributes and product-level brand attributes exist.** Some studies show that corporate-level attributes, like a reputation for innovation, expertise, or responsiveness, can account for nearly half of the reasons to purchase. This degree of influence will vary by category, of course.
- **Avoid fuzzy associations, as they hurt a brand in the marketplace.** Customers can latch onto strong value-added associations as reference

points. Without them, they gravitate to the more obvious, functional, and transient attributes, such as features and price. The lesson is: be clear, be positive. Technology companies generally have a hard time focusing on a few key associations and overwhelm the consumer with too much information.

■ **Remember that attribute importance varies by target-audience segment.** That's why you have to start with an "outside-in" customer view to determine the most important attributes – which, by the way, are not always the most differentiating. Reliability and quality are very important attributes and requirements for most brands, but focusing on these "price-of-entry" attributes alone will not necessarily create differentiation. Differentiation is having something that the competition is perceived not to have.

Customers do recognize differentiation. When you consider brands in the totality of their identity – what attributes and associations they have, their personality, etc. – customers do recognize differences. As IDG's Wave VI research, *Brands and the Buying Process*, found, customers who believe that *major* differences exist between brands ranged from 35% for desktop PCs to 61% for database software. Among more sophisticated corporate volume buyers, the numbers were even higher, from 49% for desktop PCs to 76% for database software (see Figure 7-4).

Figure 7-4

Brand Differences Recognized by Customers*

	All Respondents	Corporate Volume Buyers
Database Software	61%	76%
Portable PCs	50	65
Suites	41	50
Desktop PCs	35	49

Percentage of respondents who believe there are major differences in leading brands.

Brandness – Another Dimension of Brand Identity

The suffix "ness" means the state of, condition, or quality of being. Highly successful brands, such as Disney, Sony, and Mercedes, achieve a brand distinctiveness over time that customers come to recognize, value, and respect. In a sense, successful brands possess a quality that can be expressed as Coke-ness, Nike-ness, Patagonia-ness, Ben & Jerry-ness or Harley-Davidson-ness. This uniqueness is the sum of a brand's personality, identity, and experiences with customers.

Such richly imbued brands understand that their brandness is a vital part of their brand personality and business success. Like the brand itself, brandness is dynamic and must be purposefully managed to maintain or enhance its state of being.

A famous example of mismanaging brandness occurred in 1985. The Coca-Cola Corporation had carefully researched a product improvement that presumably would be good for the soft-drink business. They conducted extensive "blind" tests to ensure objective, "brand-less" judgments. Then, with great fanfare, they introduced the "New" Coke, which immediately caused an uproar among loyal Coke drinkers. In the consumer's mind, the taste wasn't new and improved; it was new and different. Most importantly, they didn't want a change. Coke had messed with the consumer's view of what the brand was about – a soft drink that stood for a time-honored tradition of unvarying taste. Coke recovered from this blunder by reintroducing "Classic" Coke, and, ultimately, was able to appease loyal customers and retain the unique and desirable "ness" of its brand.

On the other hand, Nike is an excellent example of leveraging brandness to successfully expand into new markets and enhance business success. After Nike announced first-quarter fiscal 1997 results, the best in company history, Chairman Philip Knight said, "Brand strength, which many thought was nearing its peak last year, continues to grow unabated." This brand growth is detailed in a *Business Week* article (June 17,1996) by Linda Himelstein entitled "The Soul of a New Nike." Nike's aggressive business expansion plans into eyeware, a variety of sports equipment and services, say a lot about Nike's ability to leverage the strength of the Nike brand. Through years of powerful communications and conscious, focused brand management, Nike has achieved an elevated state of "Nike-ness."

The Nike brand stands for "a way of life" that is best illustrated by the variety of high-profile sports superstars who appear in Nike commercials and endorse its products. This "way-of-life" brand proposition is a very broad expression of what the brand represents and is what enables Nike to confidently extend its rich brand personality and brand into so many new markets.

It's clear that most technology brands – with the obvious exception of Apple and a few others – have not yet developed a strong "brandness," but it's a worthy goal for brands of all sizes.

Brand Loyalty: Nurturing the Brand Relationship

At the beginning of this chapter, we discussed customer retention. The brand term for customer retention is loyalty. Within technology companies, brand loyalty is just now getting the attention it deserves as a management and marketing principle. Brand loyalty is an asset and needs to be regarded as such. It's difficult for many technology companies to get their minds around this idea because they are often disconnected from their customers. Since many technology companies (especially hardware manufacturers) generate most sales through indirect channels (e.g. distributors), they often do not know who buys their products and, therefore, who is the actual end customer. In addition, organizations delivering customer service and technical support are typically seen as cost centers, not opportunities to build brand loyalty. For many technology companies, then, brand loyalty is not an easy concept to grasp or do much about – yet customers, in general, have a predisposition to be loyal to the brands they buy, assuming, of course, the products perform as expected.

As discussed earlier, customers don't just buy and use technology brands; they experience the brand in different forms and fashions throughout the entire purchase and usage cycle. For all practical purposes, they have a relationship with the brand. As Larry Light says: "The opportunity to begin an enduring relationship begins with the sale. To build that relationship, we must be concerned with what happens after the sale."[10]

IDG's Wave VI research, *Brands and the Buying Process*, also examined the strength of relationships that exist between technology brands and customers. As Figure 7-5 shows, just over half of the respondents were strongly committed to or expected to stay faithful to their brands. Those were the aggregate findings. When the study examined individual brands, however, the differences were striking. A discouraging 73% of Packard Bell customers, said "Fine, but Others Also" or "Never Again," as opposed to only 10% who "Expect To Be Faithful" to the brand. Apple, as might be expected, came up with the highest number, 36%, of customers who "Want and Expect To Be Faithful" in their relationship with the brand. Some differences were less pronounced but still meaningful. For example, for spreadsheets, 60% of Microsoft Excel customers professed a desire to be committed and faithful, while only 52% of Lotus 1-2-3 customers felt the same way about the brand.

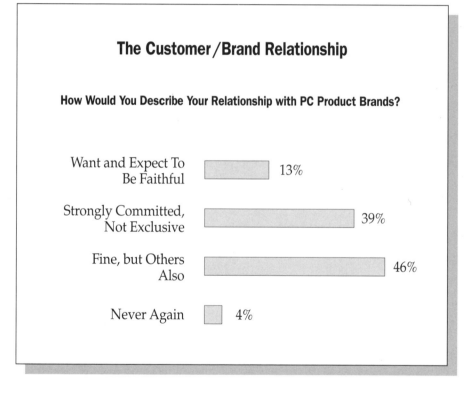

If most customers have a desire or at least a predisposition to stay with the brands they already buy, what can technology companies do to nurture that relationship and build brand loyalty? Here are some key points to consider:

- **Know who your customers are.** This basic principle is still difficult for many technology companies to deal with effectively. Registration and warranty cards, or even on-line registration, typically turn up only 30 to 40% of customer names, even when managed efficiently. Compounding the problem is the existence of different customer databases in various parts of a company. Marketing has one (or more). Sales has one. Customer service has another. Literature fulfillment keeps its own. Not long ago, a fast-growing workstation company held a meeting to discuss database consolidation, and 23 different database owners attended. Two years later, only 16 of those lists had been consolidated.

- **Know why they buy from you.** Are customers buying because of your brand-value proposition or because of other, less differentiating reasons like price? Proper research can tell you.

- **Know the value of your customers.** Not all customers are profitable customers. Here, as in most economic situations, Pareto's Principle applies: 80% of the revenue is probably accounted for by 20% of the customers. Again, research can offer insight and help target retention to the more desirable, profitable customers.

- **Keep strengthening the relationship.** You need to provide some acknowledgment and appreciation of customers in a personal manner. Offer some form of loyalty or frequent-buyer program, if feasible. And make certain you distinguish existing customers from prospective ones. For example, software-upgrade offer mailings that don't treat long-time customers or multiple-purchase customers differently from new buyers are missing opportunities to build the brand relationship.

- **Build a comprehensive database to track the relationship.** Companies which invest in technology and other resources to maintain a marketing-oriented database of customers will reap huge potential returns on those investments. Studies show that a loyal customer can be up to nine times more profitable than a disloyal one. (It's ironic that many technology companies are not as proficient or advanced as other companies in using their own technology for database management: Toyota uses a single Sun Microsystems workstation to manage a database totaling seven million customers.)

Integrated Communications

Many companies go about creating and disseminating communications in a disconnected fashion, not realizing how much each element of their communications is perceived by customers from a collective perspective.

Communications can be consistent and add up to a uniform brand presentation for customers – or they can operate independently and fail to leverage the totality of what is communicated. As far as brand strategy is concerned, the key is to think about and strive for true integration of communications, not just coordination. As Figure 7-6 shows, unless that layer of brand strategy is firmly in place and guiding all communications efforts, it's easy for planners and managers to stray from integration when faced with pending deadlines or special opportunities. Having the strategy in place is still not enough. True integration happens only when a consistent and almost cultural way of thinking about integration spans all functions and levels.

Figure 7-6

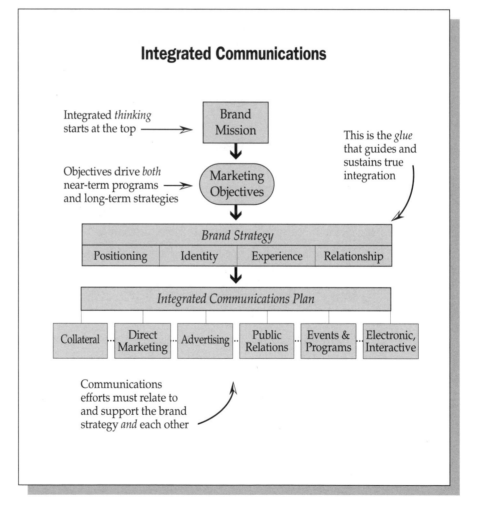

Creating a Climate for Integrated Thinking

The power of *integration* is a concept that all technology companies understand when it comes to technology, i.e. integrating various components to make a reliable personal computer or integrating various applications to make a robust software suite. Nevertheless, many fail to recognize the power of integrating branding efforts and communications. Many companies go about brand strategy in an inconsistent, start-and-stop, disconnected manner, so it's not surprising when they fail to either build strong brands or fully leverage existing brands.

Recently, Erica Baccus, formerly of FCB Technology Group, conducted a private survey of 100 marketing and marcom managers. While acknowledging the importance of integrated marketing, only 31% believed their companies were very effective at it. Given internal obstacles (most often cited as the reason for lack of effectiveness) and the pace of this industry, how can a company move beyond the mere tactical coordination of marketing and communication efforts and become more strategic and integrated in its thinking?

Pay more attention to planning? That certainly helps, but, in a study done by *Business Marketing* magazine, only 26% of companies even had a marketing plan at all, well integrated or not. Turn to the agency? From some, you're likely to hear well-meaning comments like: "Of course we communicate regularly with the other disciplines on client projects." That's not good enough. Other service agencies, generally with the words "integrated communications" in their names or marketing materials, promise one-stop shopping. Handing off this important task to an outside agency, however, is not the best approach.

It's really up to companies to deal with the integration issue. Agencies certainly have their own integration challenges, but their role is not to be the primary agents of change for clients. How, then, can you achieve the high level and quality of integration that can make a difference in how effectively and how fast you build a strong brand?

In our view, the key is *integrated thinking*. Truly effective and strategic integration comes from a state of mind – a mental condition throughout an organization that creates and nurtures an environment where all the players expect and allow their marketing and communications programs to be fully integrated. Integrated thinking helps overcome the barriers that fight integration. It encourages people to routinely plan and execute programs "horizontally" across multiple channels of communications. It requires people to consider the impact of, say, advertising on database marketing or reseller communications on end-user communications – early on and way upstream in the planning process, rather than after the fact or in isolation.

Some companies already get this and operate accordingly. Len Vickers, formerly the senior marketing communications executive at Xerox, is a proponent of integrated thinking. According to Len, "We all want integration. But you don't integrate by integrating. Downstream integration is a by-product of upstream focus – i.e. early integrated thinking. Real integration has to do with the spirit or the content of what you are saying and doing, not just the letter, the form, and the mechanics." Integrated thinking is as much philosophical as it is procedural.

Of course, integrated thinking doesn't just happen. As a marketing director or corporate communications executive, what can you do to drive more integrated thinking throughout the communications and marketing functions of your company? Clearly, you must make certain that the company is addressing the higher-level, strategic considerations, as well as the more practical steps that can create a climate for integrated thinking and lead to more rapid and successful brand development.

First of all, integrated thinking really starts at the top of an organization. Not just with management (although their support is essential) but also with a clear, empowering statement of *business* purpose and direction, which includes fundamental values that drive and guide employees in their everyday activities. A good example of such a declaration is Saturn's mission statement which makes it clear that "members of the team" (the company's term for employees) are expected to fully integrate their activities routinely. The team can't help but bring integrated thinking to both the planning table and daily actions, because employees regularly consider how to work together more effectively.

Second, having a clear statement of the longer-term *brand* purpose and direction – at both corporate and product levels – frees people to develop more creative brand-building ideas and puts proper boundaries in place to guide integrated thinking. A recent brand-strategy development project at HP took a major jump forward when agreement was reached on a powerful statement of the brand's "strategic intent," thereby enabling the company to use this declaration as a guidepost for future branding initiatives.

Third, does the company recognize that every customer contact helps build brand equity – then attempt to manage (integrate) company procedures and responses accordingly? It was recently reported that Compaq, one company which understands integration, has conducted a comprehensive brand audit to identify every contact a customer has with the Compaq brand. Using this information, the company can better understand and manage those "little moments of truth." That's integrated thinking at work.

Finally, here's a list of questions which can help drive more integrated thinking into and throughout an organization:

- Are marketing and communications goals and objectives determined before budget allocation?
- Are roles and responsibilities for each channel of communications clearly identified up front?
- Are there tight, real-time communications links between all parties – and links to their different forms of communications – so that all communications work in a more consistent, integrated fashion?
- Are measurement goals and plans established?
- Is program or campaign planning done jointly with all communications people using common tools and practices?
- Are strategy documents and creative work-in-progress reports routinely distributed to all parties?
- Are joint post-mortems done at the end of a program or campaign?
- Is there ongoing commitment to training and education for integrated, brand-building program development and management?
- Do job descriptions, performance evaluations, and incentive rewards support integrated-thinking goals?
- Do functional charters explicitly mention integration values and goals?
- Are proper guidelines in place for exploring new media and emerging channels of communications?

Integration at HP

As an example of integrated thinking in practice, the HP printer supplies group works in partnership with its agencies on a global basis. Anticipating a shift to the "razor-blade marketing model" that views selling supplies as paramount to ongoing business success, HP recently launched a major initiative to sell more LaserJet toner cartridges and paper. Company research found that competitive knock-offs were commonplace and that HP was losing out big on after-market sales. Based on these findings, the company developed a strategy focusing on HP quality. Of course, execution of this strategy is highly dependent on an integrated approach to communications.

Together with their advertising agency, Winkler-McManus, HP developed a creative and sensible integrated strategy. Winkler functions as the so-called "alpha" agency and takes the lead in formulating the communications strategy, working in tandem with the local and specialist "omega" agencies to guide communications development and execution in a variety of channels. As Agneiska Winkler says, "We manage the intellectual content of the brand."

To kick off the integrated campaign, Winkler held a two-day planning conference with the client and the "omega" agencies to determine the structure of the working relationships. A program was developed to electronically link nine different agencies worldwide, allowing all information, artwork, creative ideas, research, etc. to be shared on a *real-time* basis. Winkler set up an electronic "private-client office" that functions like a repository web site or Intranet, storing all relevant materials and learning that are accessible by password to any client-authorized person worldwide. Winkler is now refining this system to facilitate integration, including the ability to link both a relational database and customer database.

Clearly, progressive ways of working with agency partners, combined with savvy utilization of new electronic technology tools, can elevate integrated thinking to new levels. At HP, this approach works particularly well because the company's team-oriented culture fosters powerful endeavors such as this.

As the list and HP example illustrate, the difference between integrated thinking and thinking you're integrated is dramatic. The former is the all-too-rare condition that gets you to a state where strategic integration is the rule, not the exception. The latter is generally tactical coordination at best. True integration presents a unified brand identity to customers and results in a more effective use of limited budgets in building brands.

Implementing Brand Strategy

Strategy implementation is five times harder than strategy development.

–Booz, Allen, Hamilton

The compelling reason to adopt and implement *PowerBranding* strategies just discussed is simple: to build brands for competitive advantage. But sound brand strategy is not always simple to implement. Even with a thorough understanding of the brand experience, even with a well-articulated brand identity and value proposition, and even with an integrated approach, implementation can be difficult and setbacks can and will happen. As we explored earlier, technology brands operate in dynamic, shifting markets and face a variety of constraints – like relentless quarterly revenue demands and an overarching short-term focus – that can impede successful implementation. Brand-strategy execution requires discipline and fortitude; it also requires flexibility and creativity.

Sometimes the competitive situation demands brand retrenchment, as Dell wisely did a few years back when its notebook offerings were less than stellar. Other times it requires simultaneous brand repositioning and channel expansion, as Compaq recognized after stumbling briefly in the early 1990's, before significantly enhancing distribution channels and product lines while lowering manufacturing costs and slashing prices across the board. For some companies, successfully managing channel relationships and building brand-name in the channel first, as opposed to starting brand name building among end-user customers, can be an astute strategy. Why? Because, at least initially, without adequate "shelf space" many products can't get the exposure they need in order to gain a foothold in the market (over time, the Internet may minimize the importance of indirect channels, but, at least for now, only a small percentage of technology products are directly purchased via the Internet).

In addition, many companies, especially start-ups, may feel unable to invest the necessary resources to build a brand and initially shy away from brand-strategy formulation and implementation. A common misconception that a large marketing budget is required to build a strong brand discourages many smaller companies with limited resources. In fact, while ongoing investment serves to build brands, a number of steps can be taken to increase the chances of brand success without much, if any, incremental funding. We call these "high-thought/low-cost" brand-building ideas because they focus on thinking and processes that *collectively* can make a difference for companies of all sizes.

High-Thought/Low-Cost Ideas for Brand Building:

- **Focus limited resources on a tightly defined target or market.** Too many companies attempt to go after broad markets and fail to make progress because resources are spread too thin. Concentrate, get established, build – then expand.

- **Focus your communications on a few key messages.** Too often companies try to say everything about every product and every service in every ad. With so much information and competition for mind share, customers only retain a small portion of what they're exposed to, so don't overwhelm them. Stick to a few key messages – then communicate those messages consistently and repeatedly.

- **Establish clear direction and an approval process up front for major branding efforts like advertising.** It's very inefficient and expensive to keep changing direction and creative materials at the last moment because of new input. Include everyone who needs to be involved – especially senior executives – right from the beginning.

- **Develop a consistent, strategic briefing process.** This process should be designed and consistently implemented with brand-building goals and objectives in mind. Include an international scope in the planning process, too.

- **Communicate new brand initiatives widely and efficiently.** It's important to let salespeople and other employees, as well as channel partners, know what's coming and what's expected so they can capitalize on the opportunity.

- **Run surveys that compare one period to the next, or one country to another.** Often research is done ad hoc and without thinking about the need to compare results over time or across markets. Continuous or broader tracking can provide important brand-building insight.

- **Distribute research findings and insights widely and quickly.** Establish a process for summarizing important customer knowledge and brand insight – from everywhere – to all individuals with brand responsibility. That way, corrective action can take place fast.
- **Widely disseminate creative materials electronically.** Intranets create new opportunities to make good ideas available to the entire company.
- **Use the Internet.** Anyone can create a web site inexpensively. But, it takes talent, careful planning, resource dedication, and creativity to utilize the site to help build or extend a brand.
- **Harness all available technologies to leverage your brand.** The Internet, on-line services, electronic bulletin boards, inbound and outbound telephone and fax systems, and other technologies should be used to better understand how customers are reacting to your branding efforts. This knowledge can help you make appropriate adjustments to both strategies and tactics.
- **Leverage whatever you can afford to help build the brand.** Low-cost user groups (often self-supporting) can be organized to create grass-roots or community-level support for, and endorsement of, the brand. PR remains underutilized as a powerful brand-building tool, which is ironic because it can have a significant return on investment.
- **Develop a single corporate vocabulary about branding.** Every company should have a corporate lexicon to eliminate confusion about or misinterpretation of brand issues.
- **Strive for interactive, integrated, cross-functional planning.** Since you need an integrated plan, why not get cross-functional and cross-geographic participation going right away?
- **Get proper organizational support.** Review charters for the entire organization and make sure the appropriate brand consciousness is contained in each charter.
- **Pay attention to details.** When executing any program or communications effort that can potentially help or hurt brand perceptions (which includes just about everything you do), don't overlook small details – like materials sent out in response to inquiries or site preparations for customer symposiums.

As a final "low-cost" thought – and maybe even the most important: make sure – right from the start – that everything you do is done in the context of a well-defined brand-identity strategy. As David Aaker says:

"One way to be more efficient in marketing is just to do things right the first time around. It starts with getting the identity right. If you have a brand identity that works, you're just monumentally efficient."[11]

We have just examined a wide variety of approaches to brand strategy. In the next chapter, we will explore brand strategies from the perspective of how they can be formulated and implemented to provide the most leverage for a brand – and result in a competitive advantage for the company.

8
Brand Leverage

Can one brand serve both the commercial and consumer markets effectively? We felt we could get tremendous leverage with a single brand.

– JIM GARRITY, Compaq

Embrace, enhance, extend.

– BILL GATES, Microsoft

At the time, Microsoft's co-founder was referring to what the company needed to do to succeed in the age of the Internet. Yet, this prescription for taking massive action applies equally well to successfully leveraging brands in the technology marketplace. Given the industry's dynamic nature, to simply do a good job in maintaining the brand's status quo is to miss out on the myriad ways that a brand can be successfully enhanced and extended. To fully maximize brand leverage, however, you must first establish brand building as a core business function, as we discussed in Chapter 6.

If branding is seen as integral to the company, as it is at Microsoft and Compaq, it can then become a tool for market expansion, business growth, and competitive advantage. But, as in addressing other important business challenges, there are many ways to go about leveraging brands, some more appropriate and effective than others, especially at different stages in the evolution of a brand and/or market. Ongoing line extension, for example, is not prudent in every situation, since line extension of a brand does not necessary result in increased sales or greater success for the brand.

Overextension, in fact, can dilute the strength of a brand. To address this and related leveraging challenges, this chapter will explore a variety of approaches and strategies for maximizing brands.

Brand-Leverage Options

Brand leverage can be defined as the degree to which a brand can exert influence in the marketplace and its ability to take advantage of, i.e. leverage, existing brand power. It's the actual manifestation of a brand's equity – the use of brand power to competitive advantage. Since brand leverage has a strong correlation to brand equity, the stronger the brand, the more leverage it has and the easier it typically is to extend. In some industries, like automotive, strong brands such as Mercedes-Benz or Toyota are able to repeatedly leverage their brands to successfully extend into new market segments which, in turn, further enhances the primary brand. In the technology industry, however, brand leverage is not necessarily as straightforward. Technology companies offer products that are more complex and varied and, thus, far less homogeneous than, say, automobiles. In addition, the ever-changing nature of the business, the constant flow of new products, and a tendency toward brand proliferation make it difficult to devise a reliable "brand-leverage system" that can apply equally well to many dynamic situations.

A more practical approach is to first fully understand the various brand-leverage options that exist for a given company – considering its unique brand challenges, market opportunities, and competitive landscape – then adopt the best combination of tools and strategies to maximize brand potential. Several primary options exist for leveraging a brand – from simple line extension to brand creation and from brand acquisition to dynamic branding on the Internet.

Line and Name Extension

Basic line extension is typically the starting point in brand extension. While line extension is sometimes used interchangeably with name extension, we believe some important distinctions exist between the two.

We define line extension this way:

Line extension is the introduction of a related product with the exact same name or a substantially similar name, typically for the same use or a similar purpose.

Thus, for example, adding a new hard-drive model with greater capacity to a line of personal computers (e.g. "the AST Bravo LC Model 1200 now features a 1.2 gigabyte drive") is the simplest form of line extension. A more sophisticated way to extend a line is to use similar names for substantially similar products, as HP does with its "Jet" line of printer and imaging products, including the LaserJet, DeskJet, and DesignJet.

A relatively complex form of line extension involves using a substantially similar name with a suffix to describe a differently featured product. But this form of line extension can be more challenging to manage, especially in rapidly changing, short life-cycle market segments. For example, the Toshiba *Satellite Pro* is a notebook computer, as is the Toshiba *Satellite* notebook, but it offers a higher-end feature set. Since it's conceivable that a newer Toshiba *Satellite* could have a feature-set similar to an older *Satellite Pro* model still available, customers who purchase the presumably more richly featured *Pro* series might get confused and experience buyer remorse since it's reasonable to assume that the *Satellite Pro* series has a superior feature set compared to the *Satellite* series.

This potential confusion is usually avoided by the manufacturer and its reseller partners through combined efforts to maintain lower price points for lesser-featured models. In practice, however, it doesn't always work out that way, as many products remain "in the channel" even after they have been discontinued by the manufacturer. Consequently, line extension of this kind should be carefully considered *prior* to market introduction. Clearly, it requires additional management attention in order to minimize consumer uncertainty and retain brand-naming distinctions and consistency of meaning (e.g. *Satellite Pro* maintains identity integrity by consistently being both different and more robust than *Satellite*).

We define name extension, on the other hand, this way:

> **Name extension is the introduction of a product with a related name but not necessarily intended for the same use or a similar purpose.**

For example, after the success of its Dinosaur Adventure product (fortuitously released just prior to the movie *Jurassic Park*), Knowledge Adventure decided to *extend* the name "Adventure" to two other software products: Body Adventure and Undersea Adventure. While both were educational software products just like Dinosaur Adventure, they were completely different in content and use and experienced substantially lower levels of market acceptance.

The company quickly learned that the name "Adventure" was not very extendible or leveragable. Knowledge Adventure might have originally thought that each software product was related because the product experience could be thought of as an "adventure." But, from a customer perspective, a child's interest in dinosaurs may only mean that he or she would be interested in more software titles about dinosaurs. It does not automatically suggest an interest in extensive and graphic details about the human body or ocean life.

In a subsequent refocusing of the company, Knowledge Adventure released a series of titles under the brand name JumpStart. The first title, JumpStart Kindergarten, was extremely successful, and several successive titles have enjoyed similar results. This tighter focus is, according to Founder Bill Gross, "Now building brand loyalty through a range of related products that bridge the experience of early education." The previous products all shared Adventure as a part of the name, but no other logical or compelling connection existed between them. The JumpStart products are related by having a consistent name, a logical connection, and, perhaps most importantly, a logical progression (Jumpstart products begin at pre-school and will eventually *extend* through all primary grades). This is an excellent example of smart leveraging of a brand name.

If the consumer and packaged goods industries can teach this tumultuous industry anything, it's that name extensions are wrought with many pitfalls and often experience high levels of failure. In his book *Focus*, Al Ries offers both insight and an example of the risk associated with brand extension (using line extension to mean the same as our name extension, i.e. the introduction of a product with a related name but not necessarily for the same use): "In a narrow sense, line extension is taking the brand name of a successful product (A.1. Steak Sauce) and putting it on a new product you plan to introduce (A.1. Poultry Sauce). It sounds so logical. But business is a battle of perceptions, not products. In the mind, A.1. is not the brand name but the steak sauce itself. 'Would you pass me the A.1.?' asks the diner. Nobody replies: 'A.1. what?' In spite of an $18 million introductory advertising budget, the A.1. poultry launch was a dismal failure."[1]

Ries cites other examples of name extensions that venture even further from the use and/or identity of the original name: "Bic lighters. *Bic panty hose?*; Heinz ketchup. *Heinz baby food?*; Coors beer. *Coors water?*"[2] What he's referring to here is the attempt by packaged-goods companies to leverage the name (via name extension) to substantially or totally unrelated products. While, to our knowledge, technology companies have not yet attempted such overarching line or name extensions, many have, nevertheless, struggled with its proper application. IBM committed a major blunder early in the evolution of the personal computer industry by introducing the IBM PC Jr. This product was an attempt to extend the IBM PC product line and name into the home market. The use of the "Jr." appellation was an attempt to connote a smaller version of the robust business model. Consumers were not satisfied as they immediately understood it for what it was intended to be – a "lesser" version of the original and, therefore, not very appealing.

Creative Technology, Ltd. is a company currently addressing the overextension of the strong name it built with its Sound Blaster, product series. Over the years, the company has added several products that use a part of the Sound Blaster name – Phone Blaster, Modem Blaster and Internet Blaster, for example. True, each of these products is a peripheral computer device, and the use of the "blaster" appellation serves to provide some form of recognition for new products with "blaster" in their names. But there is not necessarily a logical relationship among the products – sound cards and modems, for example. From the all-important customer perspective, the appellation "blaster" may, in fact, have a confusing connotation for modem or phone-oriented products. Although users may want to have sound "blast" clearly and powerfully through their computers via "Sound Blaster" products, they may not find the idea of a "blast" sound on their modems or phone lines as compelling. As a result, they may have a negative association or reaction to this form of brand-name extension. As Knowledge Adventure discovered, brand-name extensions work best when a logical and meaningful relationship exists between the original name and subsequent versions or extensions.

Clearly, it's as important to name products carefully as it is to carefully consider line extensions. While there are no absolutes, here are some questions that should be addressed prior to extending a product name, in part or in whole, or extending a product line:

- Is there a logical relationship between the products, their usage, and target customers, beyond the mere sharing of a name?
- Does a meaningful relationship exist between the names from a customer point of view, i.e. do customers perceive naming synergy or naming artifice?
- Does the name extension reinforce key associations of the original name and avoid negative associations, thereby providing important name recognition?[3]
- Are name and line extensions arbitrary and/or the result of choosing the "easy way out," rather than the reflection of a well thought-out naming-convention system and line-extension architecture?
- Does the naming system still make sense, or does it need modification or simplification? (This is for more established naming convention systems.)
- How often and far should the line be extended and still avoid overextension? (This is for more established product lines.)

Brand Segmentation

In addition to basic line extensions, brands can be extended in a more sophisticated manner through market and brand segmentation. One can segment a market based on geography, channel, customer type such as home or business users, new or existing customers, technically proficient users or novice users, frequent buyers or occasional purchasers, and so on. Brand segmentation, then, means creating a distinct brand offering, sometimes a subbrand, to address and leverage a distinct market segment.

Just because a market can be segmented, however, doesn't mean that a new brand or a subbrand should be created to serve that market segment.

It makes sense, for example, to create a brand offering for the home computer market because consumer needs and channels are quite different from those of the business market. It doesn't necessarily make sense, however, to have distinct brands for *every* channel segment that exists. One reason is that customers shop a variety of channels and have varying needs that don't necessarily fit so neatly into such distinct categories. IBM discovered this a few years back when it created separately named bundles (or subbrands) for nearly every retail channel segment, i.e. office product stores, electronics superstores, and computer superstores. Later, IBM determined that the single Aptiva subbrand, with slight feature variations, could be successfully extended and leveraged across all retail channels.

Subbranding

Subbranding is one of the most complex and challenging forms of brand extension. Too many subbrands, as we discussed in Chapter 6, can cause customer confusion, be difficult to adequately support, and ultimately impede the progress of the corporate brand. On the other hand, a successful subbrand can provide brand leverage by not only becoming successful in its own right but also enhancing the status of the primary brand.

IBM's highly successful ThinkPad line of notebook computers serves as an excellent example. When the product was first introduced, the company was suffering from an image of "slow to market" with new technology, especially in the important and rapidly growing notebook market segment. The ThinkPad series made IBM a major player in the market segment, contributed substantial revenue to the PC division, and helped change consumer perceptions of IBM PC products in general. According to Techtel Corporation's research of consumer opinions about technology subbrands and technology companies, over two-thirds of the increase in consumer's "positive opinion" of IBM as a company could be attributed to their positive opinion for the ThinkPad line of notebook products (see Figure 8-1).

Figure 8-1

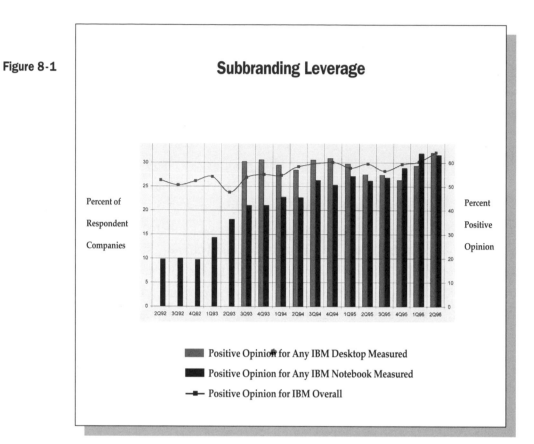

Subbranding Leverage

■ Positive Opinion for Any IBM Desktop Measured

■ Positive Opinion for Any IBM Notebook Measured

—■— Positive Opinion for IBM Overall

All indications suggest that all the small and big – and consistent – things that IBM has done with the ThinkPad subbrand over the past several years time have considerably enhanced both the subbrand *and* the corporate brand. Clearly, subbrands provide the most leverage when they are significant and successful enough to impact the larger equity of the entire corporation.

Leveraging Brands through Acquisition

Because many technology companies grow, to a large extent, via the acquisition and assimilation of other companies and their respective brands, how they deal with acquired brands is extremely important. Successful absorption into a properly construed master branding architecture can mean that acquired brands increase in value and, in turn, accrue benefit to the master or core brand. On the other hand, less-than-optimal assimilation can mean that subbrands diminish in power and perhaps negatively impact the strength of the acquiring brand.

ThinkPad: Successful Subbrand Development

IBM has consistently done almost everything right in developing and managing this particular subbrand. It all starts, of course, with delivering consistently outstanding products, and IBM has accomplished this. Take the name—ThinkPad—it's simple and meaningful. But the name was not born with meaning; IBM created the meaning through years of strong communications. In fact, originally, ThinkPad was the exclusive name for IBM's pen computing products, a market which has yet to take off. When IBM decided to use the ThinkPad name for all notebook computers, the inaugural launch campaign featured the theme line, "Use it wherever you think best," which associated the "think" part of the product name with the idea of portability. Later, new communications campaigns developed meaning for the "pad" part of the name, through a series of ad executions that played off the dual meaning of "pad" by featuring famous people using the IBM ThinkPad in their unique workplaces (i.e. Francis Ford Coppola's Pad or YoYo Ma's Pad).

IBM's smart communications have paid attention to small, yet equally important, details as well. An innovative TrackPoint pointing device is one reason the IBM ThinkPad was so successful from the outset. This small red device, integrated into the keyboard to save precious design real estate, was an instant hit among notebook users. This innovation is played up in a recent IBM ad: "Introducing the new ThinkPad 365. Because everyone could use an affordable place to think." Here, the company leverages *both* aspects of the product name. In addition, the product-name logo uses a red dot above the "i" in "Think" and the notebook photograph features the word "Think" inside the screen space, also with a red dot. These subtle cues further link communications with the product distinctiveness, i.e. the red pointing device, and ultimately enhance the product personality, the subbrand, and the overall corporate brand.

Cisco, the hugely successful internetworking leader, has adopted a very straightforward and effective acquisition strategy: Cisco is the master brand, and every company and/or brand that they acquire becomes, at most, a subbrand, subordinate to the Cisco brand. Since to date all acquired brands (products and/or companies) have been within the strategic boundaries of the internetworking business which Cisco dominates, each has consistently added to the overall strength of the Cisco brand. To a large extent, Cisco's success in leveraging each subbrand through acquisition is due to a highly efficient operation that enables it to absorb and integrate so many diverse companies and cultures, each of which benefits from Cisco's greater capabilities in manufacturing, distribution, marketing, sales, development, support, etc. Cisco is also smart in how it decides on which subbrands to retain. According to Keith Fox, Cisco's Vice President of Corporate Marketing, "If a company has a strong corporate brand name, it becomes a product line brand (e.g. Stratacom, the name for our wide-area networking switches). In some cases, the acquired product line name is stronger than the corporate brand name (e.g. Crescendo workgroup switches), so we keep the product name, as we did with Catalyst."

In contrast to Cisco's unequivocal acquisition strategy, some companies like Symantec have not been as clear and efficient in how they have dealt with brand acquisitions and implemented subbranding strategies. In addition to the Norton brand acquisition several years ago, Symantec has acquired numerous other well-known companies and their brands. In many cases, the companies (e.g. Central Point and Delrina) and/or their brands (e.g. ACT!, Fastback, PC Tools, and Winfax) have strong brand-name recognition, so Symantec has been reluctant to make the acquired brands clearly subordinate to the Symantec brand (most of Symantec's packaging, for example, gives significantly greater visual and communications prominence to product brand names over the Symantec corporate brand name). Marketing these subbrands largely as independent product brands has limited Symantec's ability to build strength and equity in the corporate brand.

In all fairness, what has also made Symantec's challenge more difficult than, say, Cisco's, is that the product breadth offered by Symantec presently reaches a much more heterogeneous target audience. By contrast, Cisco's target markets and audiences, primarily corporations and networking managers, are by and large homogeneous. This makes it easier to acquire and manage companies and their brands under an existing brand name that already has relevance and meaning to its core audience. Symantec, on the other hand, offers everything from simple products like PC Handyman, targeted at individual consumers, to more sophisticated programs like

Norton Utilities, targeted at more experienced individual and business customers, to Norton Administrator for Networks, a system-level or enterprise networking product targeted at network managers.

Lotus represents a variation of these two acquisition strategies. So far, IBM has retained the Lotus brand name as a completely *independent* brand. It has not attempted to somehow merge the name with IBM or utilize it like a traditional subbrand – i.e. no IBM logo appears anywhere in any Lotus print advertisements. From a communications standpoint, there is a distinct separation (even if customers know that IBM owns Lotus). At the time of its $3.2 billion acquisition of Lotus, while IBM had software revenues in excess of $10 billion, it did not have Lotus' brand recognition or customer loyalty in software. Nor did it have a product with the momentum of Lotus Notes. It made sense, then, for IBM to retain the unique identity of Lotus. Because some Lotus products serve different customer segments than other IBM software products – and because the Lotus brand name has tremendous equity – it would have been foolish to ignore this fact and abandon the uniqueness and appeal of the Lotus name.

The Lexmark brand represents another unique approach to brand acquisition. Lexmark was formed in 1991, when an investment group purchased IBM's Information Products division. Lexmark negotiated a five-year, noncompete agreement with IBM, as well as the right to use the IBM logo on products for up to five years. At first, Lexmark products featured the IBM logo more prominently than its own. Later, the IBM identity became subordinate to Lexmark's, and, ultimately, IBM disappeared from the brand identity. Initially, this was thought to be a smart way to "leverage" the IBM brand and help Lexmark slowly build its own unique brand identity. In retrospect, however, it may not have been the optimal branding strategy. According to Susan Gauff, Vice President of Communications for Lexmark, "In hindsight, it would have been better to have changed the name to just Lexmark on day one. It was almost three years before the IBM name completely disappeared from our products. This got in the way of building the Lexmark brand." While the IBM brand heritage is very strong, it's potentially much more effective for a newly formed company to immediately start building the new brand, rather than trying to bridge two names over such a long period as Lexmark did.

Clearly, no single branding strategy applies universally to acquiring other companies and leveraging their brands. However, these key considerations can help optimize success:

- Take a strategic, brand-oriented view of potential acquisitions, rather than just a technology or product-oriented one.
- Map out the various branding alternatives *prior* to acquisition.
- Understand the implications of each option, in both the short and long term (especially because it's difficult to change a subbranding strategy that's already been communicated in the marketplace for an extended time).
- Implement the chosen strategy consistently.
- Determine the optimal number of subbrands.
- Evaluate customer perceptions and subbrand performance regularly.
- Adjust brand strategies and tactics as required, making sure to obtain in-depth customer feedback and not relying solely on internal input to drive branding decisions.

Corporate Brand Versus Subbrand Investment

Corporate brands will be the only successful area of new brand building in the future...[4]

— STEPHEN KING,

J. WALTER THOMPSON, UK

In addition to determining the optimal number of subbrands, companies need to address *where* to invest and build equity, i.e. whether to invest in the corporate brand or in one or more subbrands. We would not go as far as Stephen King does in his comment about the growing importance of corporate brands – that the *only* brands worth building are corporate brands. But, given the leverage that strong corporate brands like Compaq, IBM, and Microsoft are providing to their many subbrands, one could argue that more emphasis should be placed on building the corporate brand in general.

Too many subbrands can either diminish the strength of the primary brand or simply not add to it. Building brand equity in a subbrand can also be unwise unless one is sure that it will endure. When and if the subbrand is phased out or merely loses market prominence, the question becomes whether or not it added to the primary brand during its existence. In some cases, investing heavily in product subbrands can cause difficulty in establishing meaning and equity for the corporate brand.

132

In the case of Novell, whether intentional or accidental, the strong equity established in the name NetWare (the product) has overshadowed the equity established in Novell (the company). And this approach poses a serious problem. When NetWare's market dominance began to erode at the hands of NT and the Internet, there was no easy way to just transfer that equity to Novell. As Linda Hayes, a former Novell Vice President, maintains, "There was historically no umbrella presence for the Novell brand. The company focused on the NetWare brand, not the Novell brand. There is tremendous equity in NetWare, but, because Microsoft has successfully repositioned NetWare as a legacy product and NT as the future, Novell is left without a strong position in the market."

In addition, subbrand management is very important in the context of overall brand management because, without proper guidelines and an agreed-upon investment strategy, battles over where to put emphasis and which subbrand deserves the most support often erupt. In most companies, everyone is fighting for their particular subbrand or cause. According to Jim Garrity, this is understandable because "The nature of product management is that it's a compartmentalized process where the product manager looks primarily at optimizing and leveraging the probability of success for that particular product line and subbrand, with little or no regard to what the relationship is of that product to other subbrands or how it might affect the core brand." This type of isolated or disconnected thinking carries a big risk: it can result in very inefficient brand management that impacts the success of both individual subbrands and the overall corporate brand.

In product categories that primarily serve business or corporate clients, the corporate brand and what it stands for is far more influential than any single subbrand might be. As Keith Fox of Cisco sees it: "In the consumer world, where there is largely an independent decision, having strong product brands can work better. Customers in our business-to-business market environment, however, are buying 'systems', they are buying the *company* and the ability to take advantage of the network and network services... Thus, having a master brand (Cisco) allows us to have different product (subbrand) lines that work together under this master brand umbrella." For Cisco, the product brands support the corporate brand and, therefore, help build equity for Cisco as a whole.

For other companies, however, it would be unwise to invest primarily in building a corporate brand, especially when existing subbrands already have significant brand-name recognition, familiarity, and allegiance among key customer targets. In Microsoft's case, the decision a few years back to begin investing heavily in the corporate brand was not done at the expense of well-established subbrands like Microsoft Word or Office – it was an additional expense. For Compaq, the 1996 decision to reduce the number of subbrands was done to provide better support for the reamining subbrands *and* the corporate brand, not to invest in the corporate brand *instead* of the existing strong subbrands such as Presario.

Since existing subbrands and the products marketed under their names create demand and generate revenues for companies, reducing the number of subbrands to an "optimal" level is never an easy decision. In addition, given the diversity of customer segments marketed to by many technology companies, it makes sense for companies to invest in both a sensible number of subbrands and the corporate brand. This delicate balancing act, combined with the appropriate brand management and brand-strategy practices outlined in Chapters 6 and 7, is the most prudent path to leveraging corporate brands and subbrands effectively.

Brand Creation

Of course, one of the most powerful ways to leverage brands is through brand creation. While subbranding is a key form of brand extension, developing new subbrands is also a form of brand creation. For some companies which have a well-defined master brand system, like Cisco, *all* new brands are subbrands. For other companies, especially those which do not have well-developed corporate brands or offer a wide range of products to a diverse set of customers, such as Symantec, brands that are created or acquired can be either new brands or subbrands. Rather than get sidetracked by the semantics of whether one is creating a new brand or a new subbrand, the important consideration is to deal with brand creation in a manner that maximizes brand leverage.

Norton, for example, is one of Symantec's core brands, because it is of core or primary importance to the company and it has subbrands that are subordinate to it. Over the years, Symantec has successfully leveraged the Norton brand name through the creation and marketing of several new products that function as subbrands to the Norton brand, such as the Norton Antivirus, Norton Enterprise Backup, and Norton Navigator. Some of these products have been more successful than others, but the strength of the Norton name (originally developed as a result of the success of Norton Utilities from Peter Norton Computing) has enabled Symantec to extend this brand to a wide range of utility products. Given this name strength when Symantec acquired the ACT! product from Contact Software International in 1993, Symantec could have decided to make ACT! a subbrand of Norton. Because the ACT! product has distinct functionality and serves an entirely different customer segment in the area of contact management, Symantec wisely decided to market ACT! as a new Symantec brand, rather than absorb it under the Norton brand family.

When deciding to add a new brand or a new subbrand, one should first determine whether a logical relationship exists between the products, their usage, and target customers – beyond the mere sharing of a name. In addition, one should carefully consider the merits of actually creating new brands or new subbrands versus the alternatives, such as extending current brands. Here's a simple checklist of criteria to use when evaluating whether or not to add a new brand or subbrand:

- Will the new brand or subbrand serve a distinct product category? (e.g. Lotus Notes software is a category distinct from Lotus 1-2-3 software.)
- Does the new brand meet distinct customer needs? (e.g. Compaq Armada notebooks are for mobile computing, and Compaq Proliant servers are for enterprise computing.)
- Is the new brand sufficiently distinct from other existing brands? (i.e. Is it more than a "lite" or "pro" version and thus deserving of its own name?)
- Will the new brand likely exist for several years – and are adequate resources available to support the new brand both now and in the future?
- Can existing brands be extended to serve new or distinct customer segments, thereby avoiding the cost of introducing and supporting a new brand? (e.g. IBM experienced otherwise with its failed Ambra line.)
- Will a new brand detract from the strength of an existing brand or diminish the integrity of the brand architecture? In other words, will a new brand enhance the corporate brand system or detract from it?

The Difference between Introducing a New Product and Launching a New Brand

In addition to deciding whether or not to create a new brand or subbrand, it's important to understand the difference between introducing a new product and launching a new brand.

Technology companies are very adept at introducing new products. They've got the drill down pretty well from a sales and marketing perspective. Make some early preview announcements to the press. Develop the web site. Plan an introduction event with splashy demos. Alert the channel. Develop sales-support materials. Brief the media. Develop advertising to support the introduction. Produce the marcom materials (generally at the last moment). Run a teaser ad. Hold the launch event with all the top execs and key alliance partners, if appropriate. All the while, it's a madcap rush to meet deadlines and produce deliverables. In fact, new product introductions are most often driven by "D&D"– deadlines and deliverables.

Launching a new brand is a different proposition, and it's harder. It starts with the realization that a new product introduction is never just a new product introduction – if it's got a new name, then it's a new brand (potentially). Or it may be a subbrand or addition to the brand family, in which case it has an impact on the parent brand or sibling brands. Smart brand thinking needs to be applied right from the start. That means doing all the necessary, tactical product-launch activities (as described prior) and adding a brand perspective to the planning process. This is especially important in many technology companies where product managers often have responsibility for brand-related decisions, yet lack adequate brand consciousness and knowledge.

Here are some of the key questions to ask early on in the planning process:

- What role do we expect this new product to play in the overall brand system – both when introduced and further down the road? Is it a short or long-term play? If long term, has a clear brand destination been established?
- If this is an entirely new brand, do we have a clear, agreed-upon

definition of the core brand-identity elements and the fundamental value proposition?

- If this is a subbrand (and most new products are), have we identified and thought through the impact of the new brand on current brand equity?
- Are we considering – in the development of supporting communications – meaningful customer-focused benefits and solutions and not just today's competitive product advantages?
- Have we considered budgeting for the launch on a brand-building investment basis, rather than just a fixed portion of expected sales revenue?
- Does the launch plan clearly identify expectations from and dependencies of the rest of the organization? Understanding how the relationship between the brand and new customers will unfold after initial purchase is especially key here.
- Are the product managers responsible for the new product launch required to bring a brand perspective to the process? This may be the most important question of all.

The key differences can be summed up like this: product launches are too often tactical and short-term in their view. Brand launches are strategic, cross functional, and longer term. Along with a pragmatic focus on product sales goals comes planning for long-term brand success – or at least allowing it to happen – from the start.

Brand Name Creation

When a company decides to launch a new brand or subbrand, there's always the question of what to call it. Once it's determined that a new name is needed, as opposed to extending a current name or line, then it is necessary to create the new name in a manner that makes sense for the product and is also appropriate within the brand system, considering all existing and related names, as well as potential future ones.

Sometimes companies take the easy way out and use a code name if it seems to be a catchy one. Or they ask employees to suggest names and make the selection by committee. Other companies opt for a more sophisticated approach and hire a naming consultant to develop the name. Compaq, for example, was created by Namelab, one such firm, and Compaq has continued to utilize consultants to name a variety of subbrands, including Armada, the name for the company's line of portable computers.

Leading consultants have devised sophisticated techniques to facilitate the selection of the "optimum" name. These methods include, but are not limited to, brainstorming scores of possible names; combining morphemes (the smallest meaningful word unit) to create a name that doesn't already exist (and is therefore more likely to be trademarkable); testing names and perceived meanings, associations, and attributes with focus groups; and engaging in linguistics analysis to assure the most broadly usable name and avoid embarrassing connotations in different languages (selling the Chevrolet Nova in Mexico was a classic blunder; while easy to pronounce, "no va" means "it doesn't go" in Spanish).

Whether a company comes up with the name on its own or utilizes an outside specialist to facilitate the process, brand-name creation is as much an art as it is a science. Some names convey meaning almost immediately, like PowerBook did for Apple. Other names develop richer meaning over time, like ThinkPad did for IBM. Key, here, is understanding that the name itself is important, but the customer experience with the product and the brand, as discussed in Chapter 7, is far more critical. As Ira Bachrach, founder of NameLab says, "Good names don't make products succeed so clearly as bad names make products fail."[5] While a name may initially create awareness, interest, or recognition, we don't fully agree that bad names alone can cause a technology product to fail. In the end, it's the customer's experience that creates loyalty to the brand.

Certainly, Microsoft has a very shrewd naming scheme for its products – Word, Office, Access, and Network. Microsoft's brand names are typically single words that also tend to represent the entire category, such as Word implying word processing. By choosing such "generic" words, some might argue, Microsoft is leaving itself open for the competition to take advantage of potential customer confusion over which "word" or "office" program to choose (as happened in the beer category when Miller Lite became so successful that competitors captured customers who just wanted whatever "lite" beer was available). But this has not been the case. This type of naming system actually provides great leverage for Microsoft, because the use of a fairly generic name enables the company to appear as the category leader even when it was late to a category (as with Word, Access, and Network). If the company can dominate a category, hardly anyone will remember or care whether Microsoft was the pioneer or the eventual leader. Microsoft's naming simplicity *and* consistency also contributes to the company's great leverage in the marketplace.

Like other successful new media companies, c/net is using a similar naming approach to rapidly build brand identity and potentially secure category leadership.

In addition to the cnet.com site, the company has created several subbrand sites including search.com, news.com, and download.com. Each of these sites serves unique customer interests and usage patterns by offering separate services that are distinct, and yet related. Because all c/net sites are linked, they collectively increase potential traffic and exposure and help build the overall c/net brand on-line. As Val Landi, Publisher of IDG's @computerworld sees it: "c/net's subbrand and business expansion strategy is brilliant. It provides different access points for the different audiences. In the new Internet world, you don't define the audience, it defines itself. The more access points to your site, the larger your audience can be. Rather than try to get everyone to one site, they can enter at search.com, news.com, download.com, etc. So whatever you're most interested in, you can enter via that site and then go to other c/net sites. They are identifying the c/net brand with all of the most *popular* functions on the web (what you use it for, i.e. reading the news, searching for information, downloading software, etc.). They are thus branding these key functions or uses and being perceived as the broad function itself."

Another reason that c/net's strategy is so potentially powerful is that brand awareness alone, as discussed in Chapter 2, doesn't grant you much leverage in the market. Brand familiarity, usage, experience, and preference are ultimately what matters. Some would argue that it is dangerous to pick such generic terms (i.e. subbrands) for web sites instead of using more clever or linguistically neutral ones. However, if c/net's sites can individually and collectively become the "default" and/or preferred site for such a variety of uses, then the company can rapidly build a large franchise. This, in turn, will further leverage the core c/net brand.

Ingredient and Application Branding

The success of the "Intel Inside" branding program has led to a variety of imitators, yet no other company has quite achieved the level of familiarity as Intel. Of course, no other technology company has invested hundreds of millions of dollars in creating a brand the way Intel did either. Regardless of expenditure, though, Intel's efforts clearly helped establish this unique method for building a brand.

Companies making computer components or "ingredients," like chips, peripherals, or disk drives, which are not necessarily visible end-products, face a significant disadvantage versus makers of end products like personal computers or application software programs. Because most customers can't see or experience ingredient products, or at least do not interact with them in a very personal or regular fashion, they are not predisposed to becoming familiar with them. To overcome this inherent disadvantage, component and peripheral manufacturers like American Power Conversion ("protect me with APC") have engaged in a variety of strategies and tactics to elevate the awareness level for their products beyond the expected, in order to build brand awareness and achieve brand preference and leverage.

Software companies have engaged in a similar practice that we term "application branding," in order to speed the adoption of products, ensure compatibility, and build brand strength. Microsoft has worked for years with its partners to ensure that their products are not only "Windows compatible" but also carry the Microsoft logo on packaging and collateral materials to decree Windows compatibility. As other hardware component vendors learned from Intel, so too have other software vendors learned from Microsoft. Part of the success of Internet products like Macromedia's Shockwave or Progressive Network's Real Audio has to do with the ease of downloading and installing software on personal computers. A key part of this success also has to do with company programs instituted to proliferate the usage of electronic logos. This form of application branding is quite powerful. Each time a user interacts with a site that is, for example, "Shockwave enabled," the brand gains another exposure and another customer experience, which help build the brand.

Interactive Branding

It would be impossible to write a book about technology branding without addressing how the Internet has impacted it. Likewise, given the constantly evolving nature of the Internet, it would be imprudent to confidently state "time-tested principles" of branding on the Internet – it's simply too new. Just like any statistic on Internet usage, as soon as you state it, it changes. Nevertheless, a number of brands virtually have been created overnight on the Internet, and it has changed the way *all* technology companies conduct business today. Consequently, some early "lessons" and useful insights can be shared to assist companies in properly dealing with the Internet as it relates to building, managing, and leveraging brands. To better understand the impact of the Internet on branding, we will first examine the brand leverage tool we call "interactive branding," then explore how the Internet has changed technology branding.

Some have called this form of branding simply "electronic branding," while others have utilized the trendier term "cyberbranding." We prefer "interactive branding" – a straightforward term that better describes the essential distinctions. This is appropriate because the brand experience on-line is, by nature, an interactive one.

We could have easily dealt with this topic in Chapter 6, because how a company *manages* its brand on-line is critical to the success of a brand. Alternatively, we could have dealt with interactive branding in Chapter 7, because the *strategies* a companies executes on-line are also key to a brand's success.

While interactive branding applies equally well to those two chapters, it's best dealt with here because, for most technology companies, interactive branding offers a powerful opportunity to further extend or leverage an existing brand. Although some companies have virtually built their brands solely on-line, the majority of technology companies have utilized the Internet to greatly enhance their level of contact with current and potential customers. Much has been written about all the advantages of a successful Web presence – from lowering the cost of providing service and disseminating both product and company information to speeding up the sales cycle and increasing customer satisfaction. From a branding standpoint, the Internet provides an unparalleled opportunity to connect with customers in a meaningful way to deepen the relationship with the brand and enhance overall brand loyalty. If not properly designed or managed, a web presence can also harm the brand relationship, because on-line visitors and customers are quick to make judgments. If their high expectations are not met, brand dissatisfaction can result.

In addition, interactive branding is not the solution for a brand that is not being properly managed and built into all other mediums. All the principles of smart branding apply to building a brand on-line, just as they do to building brands in other mediums. The best way to ensure success in interactive branding is to properly integrate it into the entire brand strategy, as we discussed in Chapter 7. Nevertheless, some aspects about interactive branding are unique to the medium, and some of the early pioneers in the interactive arena, like Poppe-Tyson, have learned a few lessons that can provide guidance to brand managers, especially those working at companies just now venturing into the world of on-line marketing.

Poppe-Tyson's "Four R" Approach to Web-Site Design[6]

Poppe-Tyson, one of the leading agencies involved in on-line marketing, offers the following principles to effective web-site design. It believes these will greatly enhance the likelihood of a brand's success on the Internet.

Responsive: Instead of just delivering or re-purposing a pile of product specifications, make it interactive and responsive to the user.

Rewarding: People should feel that their time is well spent. Too often marketing communications projects the company from an internal point of view. A successful web site puts users first and understands their desires and needs. With the web, strive to accumulate knowledge about each user's likes and dislikes – then deliver accordingly.

Repeatable: Design and create things and parts of the web that make the brand part of someone's life and provide impetus to return. Provide many reasons and avenues for coming back and re-experiencing the brand.

Relevant: Like all other smart communications, web communications should be relevant to your audience. The web design should also be relevant. Try to determine what the visitor is looking for and find several ways to engage his/her interests.

On the other hand, companies which have been on-line for years have certainly learned one important lesson: given the dynamic nature of the Internet, what works today will not necessarily work tomorrow. As Dennis Carter, Vice President of Corporate Marketing for Intel, puts it: "Your marketing solutions will be challenged repeatedly as the Internet evolves, opening up new opportunities and sweeping away previous assumptions and solutions."[7]

The New Brandscape

A few notable examples of companies that "came of age" along with the Internet, such as Netscape and Yahoo, demonstrate one of the first ways that the Internet altered technology branding: the technology *itself* became a vehicle for rapidly building brands. With the ubiquitous (although not yet instantaneous) nature of the Internet, users could simply download and install Progressive Network's Real Audio or Macromedia's Shockwave and experience the brand – in an immediate, personal, interactive, and impactful way.

Even before the rise of the Internet, shareware and electronic distribution of software had been around for quite a long time, and products such as Doom and companies like McAfee had already proven the paradigm of offering "free downloads" to seed the market and create broad market acceptance. Nevertheless, nothing has ever succeeded as quickly, broadly, and utterly as Netscape. Not only was a *major* corporation created in less than two years but also a *major* brand. As Netscape's chairman, James Clark, puts it: "It took a lot of courage to initially give away our Web browser and let people download it for free... But you've got to recognize the Internet for what it is – a massive distribution channel. So we threw a lot of seeds into the electronic wind, and they took root in organizations all over the world. That established Netscape as an instant brand name – perhaps faster than any other in history."[8]

In this new era, according to Val Landi, "The whole axis of the industry has been tilted. It's a new cosmology." It is no longer necessary to package a software product, negotiate distribution agreements, pay a premium for desirable retail store shelf space, put up in-store merchandising displays, and engage in the many forms of traditional media to gain a customer's attention. A company could avoid all that expense and compress the time it takes to move through the sales cycle – from awareness to consideration to trial to purchase – simply by building a good web site on the Internet. As Bill Cleary, a co-founder of CKS, says: "So what a web site does, and this is very important in a business-to-business context, is provide a mechanism where I can proceed from "awareness" to virtually closing the (sales) cycle... more efficiently, more fluidly."

Without having to advertise in any form of traditional media, without having to incur much expense beyond the cost of establishing and maintaining a web site, a brand can be created now. Jonathan Nelson, Organic Online's CEO and founder, agrees: "In some ways it (the Internet) has lowered the threshold to be a brand. This media is so commoditized, it's almost free." Especially compared to traditional print media, let alone broadcast television, the Internet as a medium to gain exposure offers an incomparable advantage.

True, getting potential customers to a web site has become more difficult (and costly) as the Internet has continued to grow exponentially. However, once you get someone to your site, the Internet offers a truly interactive experience that can more rapidly build a brand, based on the length, depth, intensity, and personal nature of the interaction possible. As intrusive as a television commercial can be, it's still merely a passive activity. Even though studies have proven that a high number of advertising "exposures" enhances recall, repeated 30 or 60-*second* commercials can't compare to the impact of spending several *hours* experiencing a brand on-line. As Regis McKenna astutely observed almost a year before the Internet fully exploded: "There's a new and evolving relationship that defines brand in the information age... Dialogue will become the way companies build brand."[9] Thus, the ability to engage consumers interactively and conduct what really amounts to a "silent" dialogue is a unique vehicle for creating a powerful and memorable brand experience.

Such interaction also impacts the speed with which a brand can be built. The Internet has accelerated the entire technology industry and changed not only the computing paradigm but also the branding paradigm. Due in large part to the incredible success of companies like Netscape, the brand landscape or the "brandscape" is forever changed.

Clearly, a lot of Netscape's brand strength has to due with its early entry and eventual strong leadership role in a market that virtually exploded overnight. In part, it also has to do with the daily nature of interaction that one can have with the Netscape browser product itself. Via the easy and initially free download of the product, customers can experience the product almost instantly. In addition, due to the user interface design and screen layout, the product identity is on the screen in one form or another for as long as one remains on-line. That's a lot of exposure, even if it's not an active interaction. Real Audio accomplished the same "instant" recognition for its product which was "downloaded" and installed by over 10 million customers in less than two years.

Other Internet brands, like search engines from Yahoo or Excite, also benefit from a similar frequency of experience or interaction. Every time one does a search on the Internet, which could be several times daily, it's via someone's search engine and results in another exposure for the brand. Some Internet products, like Pointcast which operates like screensaver software and "takes over" the viewing landscape upon a pre-determined period of inactivity, may even have greater ability to achieve rapid brand identity and brand strength because of the "intrusiveness" of the branding experience.

Microsoft, of course, understands this brand perspective. The browser war involves more than just winning a technology standards battle: it's about retaining Microsoft's status as the default "window" to a user's computing experience. As Steve Ballmer of Microsoft said recently in *The Wall Street Journal*, "We have taken measures to make sure customers get what we think is the Windows experience."[10] If another browser or primary user interface such as Netscape's becomes the gateway to the Internet and replaces Windows as the gateway to all computing experiences, then Microsoft stands to lose tremendous access to customer experience. This could, in fact, greatly reduce both the company's brand exposure and sales opportunities. Controlling the primary user interface is one of the key battles in this Internet age.

This chapter has explored a variety of brand-leverage options. In the final chapter, we will present further branding insights that provide additional guidance for brand builders.

9

Further Branding Insights

Most tech companies don't really understand the relationship between the product and the customer. That relationship is the seed of the foundation for a brand.

— JIM WARD, Wieden & Kennedy

We're trying to be more focused on what it is that the Apple brand really stands for. It's easy to lose sight of it. I think we had a wake-up call with the crisis that we had this year (1996). Any other company wouldn't have had anything to fall back on. That made us much more conscious of the value of the Apple brand.

— DAVID ROMAN, Apple Computer

In the first eight chapters, we have explored the foundation for technology branding and why its challenges are unique; articulated a framework for *PowerBranding* that encompasses branding fundamentals from brand mission to brand management, strategy, and leverage; and thoroughly examined the kinds of processes and practices that lead to building strong technology brands and creating competitive advantage.

In this chapter, we will examine a couple of brands in more depth than the previous chapters allowed for, as well as share reflections on a couple of other brands as viewed by the individuals who have confronted, or are confronting, branding challenges in real time. These first-person accounts provide further insight into how strong technology brands are built despite the day-to-day interruptions and constant change that characterize this industry.

In both the in-depth cases and first-hand accounts, we offer these viewpoints to augment the collective understanding of how technology brands are managed and, hopefully, provide further guidance to brand practitioners who want to emulate the smart practices and avoid the unwise ones – and know, beforehand, which are which.

In-Depth Brand Perspectives: Iomega and Saturn

As much as all of our examples serve to substantiate our thinking and theories, each is primarily used to support one or two points at most. To gain a more complete understanding of why a particular brand has succeeded (i.e. to take a 360 degree view) and examine several good *PowerBranding* principles working together, we present one detailed brand case study from this industry and one from another, each offering important lessons for technology brand builders.

The Iomega Story: Building a Brand, Not Just a Product

To fully grasp Iomega's tremendous success story and better understand how the company built such a strong, *leveragable* brand, you have to step back to a time when it wasn't so obvious that Iomega would rule the removable-storage market.

For years, SyQuest had been a profitable maker of removable, cartridge-based drives. It had such a strong following in some customer segments, such as advertising and design firms, that the SyQuest product name was virtually synonymous with the removable-media category itself.

On the other hand, Iomega, a close competitor, had run out of steam with the Bernoulli Box, its aging removable-storage device and primary revenue source. In the third quarter of 1995, SyQuest reported slightly higher revenues than Iomega (around $88 million for SyQuest versus $85 million for Iomega). About this same time, both companies launched important new products as well. Here's what one reviewer said:

"From a technical perspective, the EZ135 is the superior device. It zaps the Zip in virtually every performance category."

This quote appeared in a *New York Times* article (September 1995) on the growing interest in data-storage products. The writer compared SyQuest's new EZ135 removable drive to Iomega's new Zip portable drive. After considering the general organizational and back-up needs of most prospective buyers and carefully examining respective product features, the writer recommended the SyQuest product. More customers then chose the technically superior SyQuest product, and SyQuest continued to maintain its market lead, right?

Nothing could be further from the truth, as anyone who followed the fortunes of these two companies knows. Iomega triumphed, while SyQuest stumbled. Toward the close of 1996, Iomega's revenues were at an annual run rate of around $1 billion, while SyQuest, recovering from ongoing revenue declines and losses, was regrouping for another run at the mass market. How did this happen?

The demand for smaller, more-affordable storage solutions began to rise dramatically among PC buyers in 1995, and SyQuest was unprepared. Admittedly, the company rushed the EZ135 product to market and, according to Chet Brown, SyQuest's Executive Vice President for Sales and Marketing, "We lost a whole year of development because of it."[1] During this time, the company was more engineering than marketing oriented, focusing more on channel needs than evolving customer requirements.

Meanwhile, Iomega, a company on the brink of disaster in 1993, found brand and marketing religion in the form of a new CEO, Kim Edwards. New to the technology industry, Edwards joined Iomega in January 1994, and quickly assessed "a company run by engineers who had no understanding of the outside world." Insisting that Iomega become more customer-centric, he turned the company upside down and set out to take advantage of the growing mass market potential for inexpensive, easy-to-use storage. To accomplish this, the company embarked on a major *brand reinvention*, which ultimately affected the entire business model, from top to bottom.

While Iomega's success had a lot to do with outstanding performance in several key business areas unrelated to the Iomega brand, much of its success can be attributed to the creation of a distinctive brand identity. How Iomega was able to revolutionize the entire storage category is also a testimony for the power of branding. It illustrates some important differences between merely launching a new product and building a new *brand*. To reposition the company and rebuild the brand, Iomega followed several key steps.

Start with a Customer Perspective

The company's starting point, as it generally is with successful brands, was the customer. Iomega reportedly conducted 100 focus groups and 1,000 phone interviews with a wide range of end-user customers to better understand their needs. The company became convinced that the storage market could explode with the right product. Iomega listened carefully to what consumers really wanted in a portable-storage product and to what kind of messages would get their attention and motivate them to consider buying. Then, the company delivered the right product and the right messages to the market.

Meet Customer Needs without Over-Engineering the Product

Iomega's research found that customers wanted a storage device which was portable, easy to use, reliable, high quality, and inexpensive. So the engineering team set out to provide all that in a well-designed, user-friendly product. While the SyQuest EZ135 drive had greater capacity and about twice the speed of the Zip drive, users not only found the Zip drive much easier to install and run but also felt that it provided adequate speed and storage capacity. Clearly, the Zip drive wasn't over-engineered with more technology than customers asked for – it provided *exactly* what they wanted.

Create a Distinctive Brand Identity

From the early product-conception stage, Iomega set out to create a unique brand identity for the product. The Zip name itself was intended to express speed and simplicity. The product's color – indigo – was chosen because it stood out from the typical computer accessory. The product even had a more personal, front-loading design than previous storage products, and the new packaging, like the redesigned Iomega logo, was very colorful and approachable.

Yet, Iomega's marketing approach was not based on being different just for the sake of being different. Everything Iomega did with the Zip product was relevant to the target customers. These customers were not highly technical buyers; they were everyday consumers and small business people with unique personal storage needs. When they talked about storage data, they talked about their "stuff." As less technically sophisticated buyers, they were also receptive to communications that were light and fun, not full of incomprehensible technical jargon. The Zip product was launched with a promise – that it wasn't just basic boring storage, but "an easy way to get your stuff together."

As Tim Hill, Vice President of Worldwide Marketing, remarked in an interview appearing in the September/October 1996 issue of *PC World's Marketing Edge*, "To turn a typically mundane product into one that people want, you need to sell the solution or benefits, not the speeds and feeds." This is what Iomega did, and, in so doing, the Zip brand identity struck a very responsive chord with consumers and quickly became a very hot product.

Integrate All Communications to Rapidly Build a Uniform Brand Image

From the beginning, Iomega recognized the importance of having consistent messages across all channels of communications. The strategy team representing all of Iomega's communications partners developed a comprehensive, integrated marketing program. Hill described the approach, saying, "We make sure the messages and copy in a press release form the basis of the copy that our ad agency writes for a print or TV campaign, and that it fits into our channel marketing materials, and also rolls easily off our salespeople's tongues."

While the product advertising clearly played a key role in the product launch and generated significant visibility for Zip, public-relations efforts were also very effective in creating a buzz among more technically savvy, influential consumers. Iomega likewise benefited from the speed of the Internet as a communications medium, which helped spark positive "word of mouth" for both the product and the company. Finally, Iomega's channel programs were fully integrated, too. As Hill describes it: "Our goal across all channels, including distributors, resellers, and retailers, is to utilize the best of our partners programs to reach end users, while maintaining our brand identity and messaging in everything they do."

Commit to Building the Brand

Commitment means various things when it comes to building a new brand. First, a company must have a long-term vision. Hill stated that Iomega is interested in becoming the "Microsoft of storage" and, therefore, intends to "revolutionize the way PC users around the world think about and use storage." Second, commitment means focusing all company resources on brand-building goals. Edwards, with a launch deadline pending, reportedly sent a product design back to the engineers with a directive to change the way the Zip drive loaded because it wasn't user friendly enough. Third, commitment means adequate financial resources. Reaching the mass market takes a major investment in advertising and other channels of communication. While the traditional trade press and channel promotions had important roles to play, Iomega recognized the need to invest the funds necessary to reach a broader consumer audience and create pull-through demand for its product. The dominant spending emphasis, then, was on end-user communications vehicles.

What Lies Ahead

While Iomega has experienced tremendous run with Zip and other new storage products, SyQuest has brought in a new management team and is attempting to recover lost market share. According to Ron Brown, Vice President of Marketing for SyQuest, the previous management didn't have the willingness or foresight to meet the marketing challenges posed by Iomega. But, having painfully watched Iomega succeed while SyQuest suffered, the new team is fully aware that it's now a whole new marketing game – one that requires much more than great technology to succeed. As Brown states, "It's different now. We recognize the need to be more market focused. We're gathering our resources and coming back with new technology and new resolve. Watch us."

The market will watch, but Iomega has a big head start on SyQuest, both in the market-leadership race and the brand-differentiation race. Iomega has also built a significant barrier to competition with its strong brand franchise, which the company fully intends to leverage by continually introducing new products and aggressively expanding into new markets.

Saturn: Branding Lessons from a World-Class Brand

"The Saturn difference... isn't just about building a good car. That's done all the time. It's not just about creating a successful business either. That's done all the time. The Saturn difference really lies in the ability to do things other companies only dreamed of doing."

1990 PRODUCT BROCHURE

Technically speaking, Saturn isn't yet world class because the brand hasn't expanded outside of the U.S. However, with plans to launch in Japan soon, Saturn is becoming a truly global brand. But our world-class reference has more to do with the innovative and instructive way Saturn has gone about building its unique brand in the highly competitive automotive marketplace.

The Saturn story has been told many times. In fact, over 100,000 people from many other industries and businesses have visited the company's headquarters and factory to learn from Saturn. Although technology companies face unique challenges, we believe some important *PowerBranding* lessons from the Saturn experience should be taken to heart by technology brand builders.

Begin Brand-Building Efforts with a Strong Statement of Vision

Saturn not only had a tough challenge launching a new brand but also a rare opportunity. As a totally new company, it could lay the foundation for pre-determining brand equity over time. But to do that the company needed to articulate and establish the brand vision and values so all employees knew what they were striving for. The goal was to become "America's friendliest and best-liked car company." Among the core values guiding the brand-building efforts were *trust* and *honesty* – two things not previously associated very highly with cars and car buying. When a fundamental brand direction like this is in place and you execute against it consistently and faithfully, good things – big and small – happen. Small things such as car colors get unpretentious names like "medium red" and "blue-green." And big things like a recall of 380,000 cars can become a positive marketing event and reinforce a "we tell the truth" perception about the company.

Embrace Brand Building As a Core Competency

Saturn didn't use trendy words like "core competency," but it did recognize that brand building needed to be fundamental to everything it did. As Don Hudler, then Vice President of Sales and Marketing, said at a branding conference not long ago: "Our emphasis on brand building really started in day one where we really recognized a need to separate ourselves from GM, put the total focus on Saturn, and build that image from the ground up on what Saturn means, what it stands for, what we will do, and what the promises are for the intended buyers."

While established technology companies are likely to have difficulty embracing this approach, new technology companies getting started would do well to emulate Saturn.

Brand the Experience, Not the Product

One very smart thing Saturn did quite differently from prevailing business practices at the time was to redefine the product. Most car companies consider the product to be the car itself and, therefore, focus brand-building efforts around the tangible and emotional aspects of the "hardware." Saturn took a radically different approach, as shown in the following model.

Figure 9-1

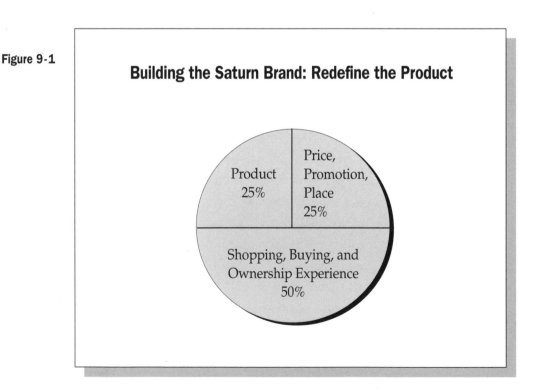

Building the Saturn Brand: Redefine the Product

154

The Saturn brand was redefined as something much more than just the product (car itself). That was only 25% of all brand and brand-building efforts. Another 25% was around the "local" issues of price, promotion, and place. And fully half of the brand was all about the experience of shopping for, buying, and owning a Saturn. It's this higher-ground emphasis on the experience aspects of the brand that has allowed Saturn to build brand equity based on the rich relationship it has with customers. This relationship is not product-based or company-based or retailer-based, but rather based on all of those levels. This focus has resulted in some powerful and sustainable competitive advantages for Saturn, even as other companies move to embrace some of the Saturn innovations, like no-hassle pricing.

Don't Just Be Different, Be Importantly Different

Branding is all about differentiation — setting your offering apart from those of the competition. The strongest brands are the ones that achieve differentiation on the dimensions that matter most to customers. To succeed, Saturn knew it needed to offer more than a good car at a decent price with a slick advertising campaign. Being a new company, Saturn was able to build in some real, tangible differences – namely, establishing a partnership between labor and management, having "team members" instead of employees, calling dealers "retailers," and offering a radical (at the time) new pricing policy based on a single-sticker price that eliminated price haggling (a part of the car-buying experience that many buyers consider distasteful and unpleasant). All of these served to provide some tangible reinforcement of the brand promise – a different, "friendlier" car experience.

All Communication Activities Are Brand Building to Some Degree

More than any other car company, Saturn lives by this principle. Working closely with its original agency, Hal Riney & Partners, Saturn makes sure that every communication with customers and prospects reinforces the brand promise. While local "retailers" still place promotional advertising, it's all done in the same tone and style as the national advertising. Collateral materials consistently support core themes of trust and honesty, while providing all the hard, factual information car-buying prospects need for comparison and selection purposes. In-store experiences are designed to help sell cars and build brand – at the same time. And some of these experiences have become the basis for Saturn commercials. The mind-set around Saturn is that this kind of integration and consistency is the right way to manage the brand, not something that has to be justified and debated on a constant basis.

A Final Thought

We could write much more about other things Saturn has done; in fact, examples pop up from time to time in this book. But, if there's one final thought to take away, it's this: fundamentally, Saturn succeeded because it took a people-centric, not product-centric approach to building its brand. Technology companies which want to build winning *power brands*, would be wise to adopt a similar branding approach.

Further Insights to Branding Challenges: Acer and Microsoft

This section contains two personal branding perspectives that were shared with us during the course of our background research. These insights from Acer and Microsoft help to illustrate a variety of smart and successful *PowerBranding* principles in action.

Acer: Following the "Six C's" To Build a Strong Brand

As we discussed in Chapter 6, a successful brand-building and management system is characterized by what we call the "Six C's" – basic principles that not only guide brand development and management but also enhance brand sensitivity throughout an organization. These include:

- **Customer focus**
- **Champions of the brand**
- **Capability**
- **Common practices and policies**
- **Consciousness of brand issues**
- **Consistency**

A couple of years ago, Acer recognized the need to build a strong brand in order to compete more effectively in the global PC marketplace. Recently, evidence of the company's efforts and commitment to these six principles started showing up in product designs and broad-based communications. We discussed Acer's brand-building efforts with Tom Henry, Director of Marketing Communications. We were interested in understanding how Acer was approaching its branding challenges. Here are Tom's, as well as Marlene Williamson's, Vice President of Marketing, thoughts on applying the "Six C's" of successful brand management.

Customer Focus

In 1995, Acer broke through the clutter of undifferentiated computer boxes by offering an innovative design that featured, among other things, different color options. Acer recognized that home PC customers are different from business customers and, therefore, open to "a fresh perspective" on design. According to Williamson, this insight led to a radical (at the time) "customer-focused" approach:

"Our goal was to design a PC specifically for the American home – not just a dressed up office (business) system. In the sea of beige boxes, which can look pretty hideous in the home environment, we look at design as a tie breaker."[1]

To this, Henry adds:

"As a company, we are now taking a consumer-needs (what consumers want) approach to product development, rather than just a technology (what we can build) approach."

Champions of the Brand and Capability

These two principles require high-level support, adequate resources, and the organizational structure and authority to make "brand-smart" decisions. According to Henry:

"There was a lot to change in a 20-year-old company (like Acer), a lot of structural things that had to go for us to have an opportunity to build a brand. There is now general agreement at high levels about the importance of building the Acer brand. Top management supports our efforts. Ronald Chwang, President and CEO of Acer America, and Stan Shih, Chairman of Acer worldwide, understand that this (brand building) is not a quick fix – it's a five-year program and major investment to become reality by the year 2000.

They feel that they have capable brand stewards in us who they entrust and empower to do what is necessary to build the Acer brand."

Common Practices and Consistency

"Our guidelines are just 10 pages...We want to navigate by a compass to head in the right direction. All 34 line items in my marketing budget are under scrutiny for look and feel, in order to help drive us towards becoming one company. The look and feel of everything from interactive CD-ROMs, to on-line, to brochures, to advertisements, i.e. across all communications, is starting to look similar."

Consciousness of Brand Issues

"A lot of (brand-oriented) counseling needs to occur on how to go about strategy versus tactics. Corporate marcom is now part of the decision-making process. I was expecting more roadblocks, but we addressed them. We are now viewed as keepers and leaders of the essence of the brand – and experts on how to approach product-based brand decisions."

Microsoft: Brand Building Is a Learning Process

In 1994, Microsoft launched its first "broad-reach" corporate-brand advertising campaign. Even though the company was already tremendously successful, it realized that it would need to build a much stronger and richer and more meaningful brand in order to facilitate ongoing growth in the years to come.

The brand-building goal was to build brand identity on a global basis and differentiate the Microsoft brand as uniquely providing the software that makes computers empowering, educational, and entertaining. The strategy was formulated around Microsoft's core strategic promise of "access"– to ideas, information, tools, fun, and even other people. At the time, Bill Gates approved an unprecedented annual budget of around $100 million and gave the managers two years to prove the investment was working.

Microsoft's brand-building initiatives have propelled the status of the company into the upper echelons of world-leading brands (see sample brand valuation and assessment findings in Chapter 4). When we discussed Microsoft's brand-building efforts with Greg Perlot, former Director of Worldwide Advertising, we were particularly interested in knowing what Microsoft had learned about brand building during the past two years as the brand was elevated to a new dimension. The following are some of the important *PowerBranding* principles and insights that he shared with us.

Establish Clear Goals Up Front and Measure Results against Them

"One thing we did right was to have clear goals for the brand that we could measure against and get people to value. Regardless of what you think about the creative or the programs, the goals are understood and valuable and we can hold ourselves to that criteria of success worldwide. This gets the discussion out of the subjective and back to quantifiable things. We have specific goals that we think drive revenue. The brand should: be an attractor and a trigger to purchase in the category, break ties in product battles, make our scale a competitive advantage, protect prices, and be consistently understood worldwide. That's what we measure ourselves against.

"As far as brand-equity measures, we look at four things in a standardized way: awareness, brand image attributes, tagline awareness and meaning, and worldwide consistency of results. Quantitative and qualitative are combined to understand each, but quantitative data is at the core and gives us our normative trends to analyze... The key is to accept this assumption: people are more likely to buy from a company they like and have good feelings about. So the brand goal is to do that. Measurement then becomes how to track familiarity and feelings. Familiarity is standard awareness tracking and feeling; we've identified 24 different image attributes that are important, including both positives like leadership in on-line and Internet and negatives like arrogance. We determine those by what's important to customers and to us."

Make Top-Management Support a Priority

"Something else we did right was commit to the goal with top-level support and a realistic budget. When Steve (Ballmer) and Bill (Gates) originally approved this program, they put a $100 million annual budget and a two-year time frame to it. That's commitment. It allowed us to not cut important corners and have a realistic chance of measuring results. When we came back after two years and showed progress against revenue-enhancing things, they said, 'OK, let's keep doing this.' The leadership of Microsoft is unique in their ability and

willingness to make big decisions and stick by them. We could have wasted two years in cheaper pilot programs or test markets before pulling the trigger and over-thought this thing. We'd be in a different situation if we were starting this now; the world would have passed us by. Nothing is more motivating to managers than that type of guts and decision-making."

Recognize It Will Take Time to Get the Organization Behind the Program

"There is a sensitivity and respect now about the value of the Microsoft brand that didn't exist two years ago. Microsoft is a product-driven company; we don't want that to change. There is always a fear that style will come before substance, and sometimes the word 'brand' exacerbates that fear. What's true is that our people understand that having the Microsoft name on your product gives it a better chance of selling than not — we have incontrovertible data to back this up.

"We're past the point of resistance to a strong/focused brand and the money/work it takes to build that. Now, we're on to the job of getting people to think of the Microsoft brand as a relationship and not an advertising program. And that relationship is deposited through everything we do. We're trying to get people to focus more on the bond we're trying to create between Microsoft and the user. The brand promise is 'access,' and when people understand that vocabulary and incorporate it into their work, then it works right."

Think of Brand as a Relationship That Evolves, Changes, and Grows

"Another thing we did right was to have a meaty promise and be willing to be flexible about how you bring it to life. Our relationship with consumers is a living thing; we change, they change, opportunities change. So we didn't hold ourselves to one rote approach that we had to implement and stick with. We felt like there needed to be both static and dynamic parts of the brand. Building the brand wasn't a matter of creating an ad campaign and a common art direction template for everything. It needed a heart that would make us more secure to be dynamic in the implementation. To try things, make mistakes, and zero in onthe most powerful approach — just like how we build products.

"We talked about our brand being a relationship, so ultimately the brand should inspire trust. It should also inspire your emotions a bit. Technology rocks; that's our personality. It took us 18 months to dial in to the real voice of Microsoft. What we realized is our voice is linked to our products — our identity was comfortably rooted in the cool things our products can do."

Strive for True Integration; It Makes a Big Difference

"Integration has two parts: messaging and execution; a common proposition and spirit ("Where do you want to go today?"), combined with a lot of design tools and executional elements in a systematic way that gets us 80% there. What we found over time was that everyone wants to leverage; it's more efficient. So having the tools was the thing. We found you can create much more creativity and willing compliance through giving people good creative and turn-key presentations (to help them explain to their people), art work, templates, and access to helping hands, than you'll ever create through top-down decisions.

"We're very good at this now and have actually systematized much of this — it feeds on itself; when the creative is great, everyone wants to use it. It becomes uncool to have bad creative so this naturally ties everything together. Our packaging, direct mail, advertising, and product interface are working together pretty well. Advertising is serving as lead for communications and advertising is inspired by the products, so it all comes together naturally."

Final Thoughts

As we said in our introduction, our desire in writing this book was to present a practical *and* strategic approach to building and managing technology brands that could help companies of all sizes.

Given the increasing difficulty of sustaining true differentiation on product capabilities alone, we felt that detailed guidance for successfully managing technology brands for competitive advantage was more urgently needed than ever. As we discussed in Chapter 2, companies make *products*, but customers buy *brands*. In many respects, branding is not optional. It happens – for better or worse. It's what companies choose to do about it that makes the difference.

That's why possessing the necessary knowledge and having adequate tools are often just the beginning of the brand-building challenge. As we've discussed, an organization must have the foundation, direction, and commitment to brand building in order to be successful. And it has to have individuals with the ability, conviction, fortitude, and authority necessary to engage in the day-to-day battles that arise over brand building in order to really make a difference in the long run.

Linda Hayes, Vice President of Marketing at PGP, and the former Vice President of Communications at Novell, Zenith, and Motorola, sees the challenge this way:

"You have to be strong as hell to lead marketing. If you don't have the strength of your convictions and if you can't drive (it), you'll merely be a ping-pong ball, bounced around at the whim of one technical manager or another. So, you're the expert, allow for discussion, but don't back down on your principles."

And David Roman, Apple's Vice President of Corporate Advertising and Brand Marketing, views a brand and the ongoing brand-building challenge like this:

"A brand is complex and you build it over time. A brand is not what you say or even what you do; it's the accumulation of all things you've done, all of the perceptions people have had, all of your communications and customer experiences over a long period of time. You can't look at it (the brand) in isolation.

Some things reinforce the brand and some diminish it, and yet, bit by bit, you build it a little more over time."

No one ever said the fight would be an easy one; but, ultimately, it can be a very rewarding one. So go forth and make it happen.

Chapter Notes

Introduction

1. David Arnold, Ziff-Davis Boards, Aspen, December 1993

Chapter 1

1. David Arnold, discussion at IntelliQuest's Brand Tech Forum, October 1993.
2. For a more in-depth discussion on the limitations of the "build it and they will buy it" technology marketing mentality and a comprehensive analysis of the unique market dynamics that often determine why technology companies succeed or fail, see Geoffrey Moore's two outstanding books: *Crossing the Chasm* and *Inside the Tornado*.
3. Panel discussion at IntelliQuest's Brand Tech Forum, October 1996.
4. This concept was inspired by a conversation with Bob Brown, September 1996.
5. For a more detailed examination (beyond the brand aspect) of the perceived total product and how it relates to the marketing of technology products, refer to *The Marketing Imagination* by Theodore Levitt (chapter 4), *Relationship Marketing* by Regis McKenna (chapter 4), and Geoffrey Moore's two books cited above.

Chapter 2

1. Webb McKinney, Hewlett-Packard, *Fortune* magazine (March 4, 1996).
2. Dennis Carter, Intel Corporation, *Fortune* magazine (March 4, 1996).
3. IntelliQuest's Brand Tech Forum, October 1993.
4. ibid.
5. Dell virtually pulled out of the portable market in 1992, and re-entered when management determined it again had a competitive product offering. Dell has since steadily gained market share and, in a recent quarter, reported large sales increases and a gross margin improvement, partly attributed to successful notebook sales. For more insight on this, see Figure 4-5 and related discussion.
6. Presentation by Geoffrey Moore, "Branding: Beyond the Chasm," at IntelliQuest's Brand Tech Forum, October 1995.
7. For an example, refer to *Financial World* (July 8, 1996).
8. David Aaker and Robert Jacobson, "What's in a Name: The Stock Market Reaction to Brand Equity," March 1993.

Chapter 3

1. David Aaker, *Building Strong Brands*, page 343.
2. Bill Packard, *The HP Way*, page 82.
3. Panel discussion at IntelliQuest's Brand Tech Forum, October 1996.
4. Discussion by Christine Hughes at IntelliQuest's Brand Tech Forum, October 1995, and follow-up discussion with the authors.

Chapter 4

1. *Financial World* magazine (July 8, 1996).

Chapter 6

1. David Aaker, *Building Strong Brands*, page 241.

Chapter 7

1. John Scully, *Odyssey*, page 300.
2. Terry Vavra, *Aftermarketing*, page 89.
3. *Direct* magazine (November 1996).
4. *The Quest for Loyalty*, edited by Frederick Reichheld, page 167.
5. Tom Peters, *Liberation Management*, page 737.
6. David Aaker, *Building Strong Brands*, page 95.
7. Jean-Noel Kapferer, *Strategic Brand Management*, page 21.
8. David Aaker, *Building Strong Brands*, page 68.
9. Lynn Upshaw, *Building Brand Identity*, page 188.
10. Larry Light, *Ad Age*.
11. David Aaker, *SUPERBRANDS* magazine (October 18, 1993), page 35.

Chapter 8

1. Al Ries, *Focus*, page 16.
2. ibid, page 17.
3. David Aaker, *Managing Brand Equity*, page 233.
4. David Aaker, *Building Strong Brands*, page 107.
5. *Fast Company* magazine (October/November 1996), page 38.
6. Conversation with Dave Carlick, Executive Vice President of Poppe-Tyson, October 1996.
7. "The Future of Interactive Marketing," *Harvard Business Review* (November/December 1996).
8. *U.S. News & World Report* magazine (January 15, 1996), page 51.
9. Regis McKenna, *Harvard Business Review* (July/August 1995).
10. *The Wall Street Journal* (December 5, 1996).

Chapter 9

1. Interview in PC *World's Marketing Edge*, Lee Doyle, Editor (May/June 1996).

List of Figures

Glossary

Affinity	As defined from a brand viewpoint: an attraction to or liking of the brand. This liking impacts both consideration for the brand and the loyalty that can develop for a brand over time.
Attributes	The specific and different dimensions or aspects of a product that a potential buyer selects and uses to make judgments about the benefits of product alternatives. Attributes can be functional or intangible and have varying degrees of importance to different people.
Awareness	The ability of a potential buyer to recall or recognize a brand name. It is the first basic step in the purchase process. Unaided or spontaneous awareness is more desirable than prompted awareness.
Brand	The tangible product plus the intangible values and expectations attached to the product by the customer or prospect.
Brand Building	The systematic process of understanding and managing the perceptions and experiences customers have with a brand in a manner that creates added value and preference over competitive alternatives.
Brand Equity	The advantages (if any) that come from the unique set of real and/or perceived distinctions and values customers attach to products.
Brand Identity	The names, symbols, brand personality, associations, and attributes that provide the cues and messages customers use to define and understand what a brand is really all about.
Brand Image	A selective set of associations people have about a brand. Image is the way a customer imagines, perceives, or believes a brand to be.

Brand Loyalty	The degree to which customers are loyal to the brand, as expressed by their ongoing endorsement and repurchase of the brand and by their degree of support and allegiance to the brand, considering all available alternatives.
Brand Leverage	The degree to which a brand can exert influence in the marketplace and the ability to take advantage of, i.e. leverage, existing brand power.
Brand Management	The on-going process of understanding and actively influencing the perceptions, expectations, and experiences customers have with a brand.
Brand Mission	The internal statement of purpose, or reason for being, that drives and guides all activities shaping customer perceptions and experiences with the brand.
Brandness	The unique quality or state of being achieved by successfully differentiated brands.
Brand Personality	The aspect of brand identity that reflects the persona of the brand. Its components include the character, nuances, images, and feelings created and evoked by the brand.
Brand Positioning	The memorable and differentiating idea about a brand that customers/prospects have in their minds. People position a brand based on their experiences and perceptions.
Brand-Value Proposition	The strategic statement that sums up the specific quality and nature of the relationship between the brand and the customer. It is the statement that sets a brand apart from its competitors and drives purchase decisions.
Business Model	The system a company uses to deliver value to customers. It can include outside resources. It can be a competitive advantage or weakness depending on customer needs or market situation.

Channels of Communication	Any means that can be used (and generally controlled) to deliver messages to customers and prospects. Included are the media (advertising and the press), mail, telephone, Internet, sales force, trade shows, in-store displays, etc.
Consideration	The stage in the purchase process when a customer actively (but not always rationally) compares the advantages and disadvantages of several alternative (and generally acceptable) products prior to making a purchase decision.
Consideration Attributes	The specific and different dimensions of a product that a customer selects and uses to make judgments about product alternatives. They can be functional and tangible or intangible.
Familiarity	Having some understanding, recognition of, or experience with a particular brand.
Line Extension	The introduction of a related product with the exact same name or a substantially similar name, typically for the same use or a similar purpose.
Name Extension	The introduction of a product with a related name but not necessarily for the same use or a similar purpose.

Index

Symantec, 130, 131, 134
Symbols
    as part of brand identity, 102
Symbols, 116

Taylor, Jim, 102
Techtel, 127
        Demand Management System, 52
The Wall Street Journal, 84, 145
Thoman, G. Richard, 84
Toshiba, 28, 83, 123
        Satellite notebooks, 123
Total Research Corporation, 32
Toyota, 112, 122
Trout and Ries, 97

Upshaw, Lynn, 23, 105

Vickers, Len, 114

Waitt, Ted, 42
Ward, Jim, 147
Williamson, Marlene, 157

Winkler, Agnieszka, 116
Winkler-McManus, 116
Wunderman, Lester, 89

Xerox, 114

Yahoo, 27, 72, 73, 143, 145

Zappacosta, Pierluigi, 95